with blessing
Paramahansa Yogananda

S.R.F. Clerk
San Diego, Calif
Oct 17th 1968.

I Became My Heart

Stories of a disciple of
Paramahansa Yogananda:
Leo Cocks

(Compiled and Edited by Paul Gorsuch)

I Became My Heart
Stories of a disciple of Paramahansa Yogananda: Leo Cocks

Copyright © 2013

ISBN: 978-0-9890240-0-6

Library of Congress Control Number: 2013935053

Published by:
Contact Approach Publishing
San Diego, California USA

Paramahansa Yogananda

FROM SONGS OF KABIR

It is the mercy of my true Guru that has made me to know the unknown;

I have learned from Him how to walk without feet, to see without eyes,
to hear without ears, to drink without mouth, to fly without wings;

I have brought my love and my meditation into the land where
there is no sun and moon, nor day and night.

Without eating, I have tasted of the sweetness of nectar;

and without water, I have quenched my thirst.

Where there is the response of delight, there is the fullness of joy.
Before whom can that joy be uttered?

Kabir says: "The Guru is great beyond words, and great is the
good fortune of the disciple."

- Rabindranath Tagore

CONTENTS

Preface 1

Foreword 5

1: Leo's Soul Awakens 11

2: Leo Determines to Become A Monk 27

3: Leo's First Lessons as an SRF Monk 39

4: Leo Gains Insight Into His Guru and His Disciples 57

5: Leo's Guru Shows Omnipresence, Discipline and Love 79

6: Yogananda Protects, But Knows His Time Is Short 97

7: Leo Holds Vigil After Master Leaves the Body 109

8: Epilogue: Leo Re-commits to his Guru and to Living in Spirit 123

PREFACE

A true guru is one who has attained final liberation and returns to earth to serve humanity and lead receptive souls back to their eternal home in Spirit. Paramahansa Yogananda was such a guru, and like a diamond of uncountable facets, he continuously reflected the infinite light of Spirit into this world. Those disciples who are in tune with him absorb that light into their hearts and are forever changed. One of these disciples was Leo Cocks. Through this collection of his stories and letters from Yogananda and others, we get a unique and very personal view into what it means to be with a God-realized master.

At their first meeting, Leo was overwhelmed by the recognition that Yogananda was his guru. He was so filled with love that, as he put it, "I became my heart… my heart had wings and I flew up out of my body." From that moment on, Leo was utterly devoted to his guru. And like a parent who must guide a willful child so it will grow and fulfill its destiny, Yogananda guided Leo with love and discipline.

After Yogananda left his body, Leo began to share his stories of the master with interested seekers. As one devotee wrote to Leo in response: "Your stories have touched me and many others. We all have the opportunity to share in the tender care and love that Master (Yogananda) freely gave through the window of your eyes and the footsteps of your memories. I will be forever grateful to you for that unique and precious gift. Through it I have seen and felt God's love in a much deeper way."

I found the spiritual path in my early twenties. And though it was years before I realized the magnitude of this blessing, I soon found myself meeting some of Yogananda's close disciples who had known the master in the body. I met Leo and his wife Marcelle in the late 1980s when they attended the Self Realization Fellowship temple in Richmond, California. Hearing Leo's personal stories gave me a deeper understanding of Yogananda and the light he brought to this world. A deep soul friendship quickly developed with Leo and Marcelle.

Eventually, we became a family of kindred souls, and I realized that the devotion Leo felt for his guru would be his lasting footprint in the sands of time.

Still, I never thought that I would play a role in preserving and publishing Leo's stories until very shortly after Marcelle's passing in 2006. Leo had never allowed all of his stories to be recorded, and I realized there was now no one else to do it. I struggled with the responsibility of this project, feeling I was unqualified. I was an airline pilot, not a writer. I knew nothing about publishing. I had never even learned to type.

Leo didn't make the process easy. While he never overtly refused to let me record the stories, neither did he cooperate. For years there was always some excuse, some reason why *today* was not a good time. I understood part of his resistance, however. He wanted to wait until his health improved and his memory was more clear. He wanted his stories to be perfect. But as the years passed, his health continued to decline and the accuracy and depth of the details he remembered began to fade. It seemed I had been given an impossible task.

Finally, after years of effort and with time running out, I was able to make audio recordings of Leo telling his stories. It turned out to be the last year of his life. Just before he died, in early 2011, Leo was able to read part of this collection transcribed in its near-final form. He said he was pleased with what he held in his hands.

Leo was blessed for more than three years to be with an avatar, a fully liberated soul who returns to earth to help others. Yet Leo also struggled with the same burdens and challenges that we all experience. And so this account reveals the character flaws and obstacles in the consciousness of a striving disciple.

Sometimes Leo called himself "a fallen Virgo" in reference to his astrological birth sign and his awareness of his shortcomings. He once told me that he always felt that he had been more advanced in previous lives, although he couldn't spell out any specifics. He said, "I made a big mistake and I fell. But Master's hand came out and caught me so I didn't fall all the way down." Leo knew his guru loved him.

He would tell us: "Master poured out his love to me, even though he saw all the other stuff and he knew I would be leaving the ashram." And then the words would stop as his eyes filled with tears of gratitude and love. Though his guru's discipline could be fiery, Leo threw himself at his guru's feet, knowing he was loved unconditionally by someone who saw the whole of him and made him feel worthy of God's love.

I was once given a letter that beautifully illustrates this point. It tells the story of a man who lived near Yogananda's Mt. Washington headquarters. The man was not a follower of Yogananda or Self Realization Fellowship, but he met Yogananda as a neighbor who exchanged pleasantries during his walks around their mountaintop neighborhood. One day, Yogananda stopped to talk with him and the neighbor poured out his heart to the great Master, as many souls did when they felt the unconditional love and peace that emanated from him. He told Yogananda about his life and the burden he carried as a gay man in the 1940s. The master listened patiently without comment as the neighbor continued. After the man concluded, Yogananda smiled and spoke words that left a lasting impression for the rest of the neighbor's life. Yogananda said: "Each flower has to unfold in its own way."

I want to thank those who helped bring this project to completion. The three and one-half hours of audio recordings were transcribed by Bill Demorest and the letters by Menard Malaca. Eric Estep contributed inspiration, the foreword, and the paintings of Master and Christ. Kwi Cocks provided the space and focus to transform her husband's memories into written material that could be shared. The manuscript was edited by Anne Marie Welsh. I am especially grateful for the guidance and encouragement of Antoinette Spurrier, as this book would have never come into existence without her. My sincere gratitude also goes to my guru, Paramahansa Yogananda, for arranging that my part of this work would be accomplished near his desert retreat. To be able to work on this book in such close proximity to where Master wrote his sacred scriptures will always be a blessed memory.

Although I had to perform some minor editing to make the stories readable, for the most part these stories are in Leo's own words. I offer *I Became My Heart* in the hope that it will uplift all sincere seekers, showing the eternal truths that exist in the guru-disciple relationship.

A portion of the proceeds of this book will flow to Self Realization Fellowship to further the ideals that Yogananda and Leo held so dear.

Paul Gorsuch
December 2012

FOREWORD

Paramahansa Yogananda teaches that the guru-disciple relationship is the foundation of the spiritual path, that to know God we must be guided by a guru who has himself fully realized his oneness in Spirit. But how does one recognize such a guru? There is a saying in India: "The guru is known by the caliber of his disciples." I was fortunate to meet many of Yogananda's most advanced disciples––great yogis whose lives exemplify his highest spiritual ideals, who have themselves attained inner freedom through their attunement with the master.

Not all of the disciples who were with Yogananda were saints, of course. Like most of us, many were still struggling with their lower natures under a heavy load of karma. Some were doing well, some not so well. I gained understanding from all of those I met, and discovered that some of my deepest insights and greatest inspiration came from those who were struggling the most.

One such disciple, Leo Cocks, became a close friend. He was a wonderful teacher, not in any formal sense, but through our friendship and his desire to share his experiences of the master, I learned important lessons about the guru-disciple relationship and the meaning of divine love.

Everybody knew Leo. He made a big impression wherever he went. Indeed, he was big in every way. A bodybuilder in his youth, he still lifted heavy weights in his sixties and had a massive chest and arms, a big buddha-belly, big appetites, a big personality, and a big heart. He was generous with his money, his time, and his opinions, which he delivered with great exuberance. And Leo loved to get a small group around him and tell stories about his experiences with the master. Often, as Leo shared his deeply personal memories with us, we were moved to tears as Master's presence became a tangible reality for us, seeing Master through Leo's eyes, feeling Leo's devotion for his guru, and experiencing Master's love for us. In those moments I understood what Jesus meant when he said, "Where two or three are gathered together in my name, there am I in the midst of them." Jesus was speaking for all Christ-like masters.

My wife and I met Leo and his wife Marcelle at the Self-Realization Fellowship Richmond Temple shortly after we arrived in the Bay Area in 1988, and we established an instant rapport. We got together regularly over the next eight to ten years, until they had both moved to Southern California. Although Leo was well known and well loved, he had only a few close friends. For he could be difficult to be around. Over the years he managed to alienate almost everyone who was close to him. Since Leo never pretended to be anyone other than who he was, he blew away those who had idealized preconceptions of what a direct disciple of Yogananda should be like. Leo was an advanced yogi who emanated an aura of spiritual purity. But he had a personality that could roll right over other people without having a clue how much he was hurting them. There was a sweet childlike innocence about him, and he could be childish, defensive, and self-absorbed. He told his stories with a deep humility, yet he enjoyed being the center of attention. Leo's personality gave vivid expression to both sides of his nature, the human and the divine.

The fact that Leo had human failings did not bother me. I was not perfect, after all, so why should I expect anyone else to be? I found Leo to be all the more inspiring because of his flaws. The more I got to know Leo and became aware of some of his outrageous behavior, the more respect I had for him. For unlike so many devotees who, failing to live up to their spiritual aspirations, pull away from the guru out of feelings of guilt and shame, Leo held all the more tightly to Master. With utter faith Leo would prostrate at Master's feet asking for forgiveness. His despair drove him into Master's arms. For Leo had no doubt that Guruji loved him unconditionally and would always guide and protect him no matter how many times he failed, no matter how far he strayed. Daya Mata pointed out that one of her most difficult tasks was convincing devotees they were worthy of God's love. Knowing Leo helped me to understand more deeply that Master accepts us just as we are.

Leo desired with all his heart to be a good disciple. All he really wanted was to please Master. But without Guruji being physically present to discipline him, he found it almost impossible to break free of self-destructive patterns. This is the challenge we all face now that the master is gone from this world. Leo did the best he could. That is all any of us can do. And Master tells us that is all God expects of us.

I saw how Guruji protected and cared for Leo. Marcelle told me that she was only with Leo at Master's behest. When they first met, Marcelle fell deeply in love with Leo, "swept off my feet," as she put it. But Marcelle had doubts about marrying him. Leo was insistent, however, and Marcelle began to feel Master urging her to accept Leo's proposal. She prayed for further guidance, and Daya Mata came to her in a dream and confirmed her intuition. Then she asked Brother Anandamoy about the dream. He reassured her that it was a true superconscious experience, and that without her by his side for spiritual support, Leo would not have the strength to remain on the path. Marcelle accepted her role joyfully, but, as it turned out, at great personal cost and sacrifice. She was a truly wonderful, pure-hearted soul, and knowing her is one of the great blessings of my life.

The spiritual path is long and hard. Longer and harder than we can imagine. We are burdened with karmic tendencies from a distant past we can no longer remember. We all have our failings, our regrets, our periods of despondency and self-doubt. We all fall, again and again. Those who progress on the path are those who never give up, who get back on their feet and keep going, no matter how hard it gets.

Leo never gave up. He never lost his connection to his guru, and Master watched over him to the end. When Marcelle became ill, Master sent Leo another angel, Kwi, to help him take care of her. After Marcelle's death, Kwi stayed with Leo and became his wife, caring for him night and day until he passed away several years later.

Guruji had promised Leo that if he remained faithful, he would be there when Leo died to welcome him into the next world. Leo looked forward to that day when he would be reunited with his beloved guru.

Seeing how tenderly Master cared for his wayward disciple in life, I have no doubt that Master was there for him at death. And this same promise Master gives to all his disciples. No matter how difficult our tests, no matter how many times we fall, if we never let go of our guru, he will never let go of us.

When Leo told his stories he was reliving those three and a half years he was with the master——that extraordinary experience of being with an avatar. After Guruji passed and Leo left the ashram, the world and its temptations gradually dragged him down from the spiritual heights he had attained. The retelling of those events with his guru became Leo's way of keeping his memories alive, dynamically recreating the experience of Master's living presence here and now, for himself and for us.

During the years in the Bay Area, I asked Leo if I could tape his stories. He always said no. And I understood why. These were his stories, his lifeline to the guru, and they were his to share in the inspiration of the moment. He wasn't ready to give them away. So I am grateful to Paul Gorsuch for his dogged determination against all odds to get so many of Leo's stories recorded during the last months of Leo's life. And then in taking on the project of publishing them, with Leo's blessing, for the inspiration they will provide for all the devotees.

Eric Estep
April 12, 2012

PARAMHANSA YOGANANDA
Founder

PUBLISHERS
Self-Realization Magazine

SELF-REALIZATION FELLOWSHIP

CABLE: "SELFREAL"

International Headquarters

PHONE: CApitol 0212

SAN RAFAEL AVENUE • MOUNT WASHINGTON ESTATES • LOS ANGELES 31, CALIF.

26th Jan - 1951

Dear Leo,

It is you showed full devotion & wrote me to fully go on the path. Now when tests come you weaken — that should not be.

It is only 100 P.C. going all the way until death proposing. Kriya & duties assigned that you reach God.

I have forgiven you, but you must not be fickle or waver. Do your daily thinking of God all the time — coldness will do you no good. I have forgiven you — you must forgive yourself. All my love

P. Yogananda

9

Dear Leo,

It is you [who] showed full devotion and wrote me to fully
go on this path.

  Now when tests come, you weaken - that should not be.

  It is only 100 percent going all the way until death, per-
forming Kriya and duties assigned that you reach God.

  I have forgiven you, but you must not be fickle or waver.
Do your duty, thinking of God all the time - coldness will
do you no good.

  I have forgiven you - you must forgive yourself.

  All my love,

Very sincerely yours,

P. Yogananda

LEO'S SOUL AWAKENS

Leo Cocks and his family are already schooled in San Francisco in Vedanta, a group of Hindu spiritual philosophies derived from the Upanishads of ancient Vedic texts. Through his mother, Leo hears of Indian yogi Paramahansa Yogananda's work, and soon meets him in San Diego, California. As his soul is shaken awake, Leo becomes his heart. Though he must leave for U.S. Navy sonar school in Key West, Florida, Leo takes the "Renunciate's Vow" in which he makes his monastic intentions clear. His beloved guru Yogananda praises Leo for making room for God in his life.

LEO MEETS HIS GURU

I always had an interest in philosophy. I grew up in San Jose, California and my family started going to the Vedanta Temple in San Francisco. In three years of study of Vedanta, I learned about Ramakrishna, reincarnation and the masters and saints. Later, I went to Navy boot camp in San Diego and applied to sonar school. While in San Diego, I received a letter from my mother telling me about two friends of hers who were originally from the Encinitas area. They moved to San José, met my mother and they told her about Yogananda and Self Realization. They told my mother to write to me and suggested I check out Yogananda. They told her I could find out what I thought about it. My mother then told me, so I received this all secondhand.

On Sunday, October 17, 1948, I went to the San Diego Church (Temple). I'd never seen Yogananda before. I never read a book or heard a lecture of his. I knew absolutely nothing about him. I was sitting about three quarters back from the front of the church. He came out and we stood up. He prayed, he chanted and then he had a little talk before the meditation. As soon as he did that, it was just like everything opened up! I became my heart, my chest opened up, my heart had wings and I flew up out of my body about eight or ten feet. I could see him, and I instantly just felt, "Oh, He is my guru! He is my guru!" And I thought, "Oh, at last I found him again!" That was when I knew he was an avatar. That feeling of expansion lasted for a quite awhile and then I came back to normal.

After the service, I saw that there were people going up to him and getting blessed. I got in the line. He blessed me and asked me about myself. I talked a little bit, but it was hard to talk because I was all choked up. He said, "I want you to follow my teachings." Then he told me, "I want you to write to me." I couldn't figure that one out. Why does he want me to write to him? I am going to see him every week; San Diego Church one week and Hollywood the next. Why do I have to write to him? But he saw it differently, I guess. Standing there with Master was the future Brother Bhaktananda (at that time his name was Michael). Master said, "Michael, you help Leo. Afterwards, you go in the back, with the teachings and the books and things." So Michael and I went to the back of the chapel and he pointed out each one of the books. He showed me the lessons. I just said: "That's great, give me everything." I signed up for the lessons and I bought a copy of all the books Master had at that time. Michael must of thought: "This guy is crazy!"

I didn't know I was going to need everything because it turned out I wasn't going see Master again for a long time. I was immediately transferred to Florida to go to sonar school! But he knew all that before I did.

I was blessed to have my mother and step-father (the Andersons) and my brother (Ivan) on the path with me. Master would write to them also. My Mother would share his letters with me by hand copying them and sending them to me.

August 8, 1949

Dear Mrs. Anderson:

Thank you for your two recent letters, which reflect so dearly that wonderful love and devotion for God which I have always seen in you.

I feel that Ivan's decision to go ahead is a big step forward, and I have complete faith that if he will continue and see it through, always inwardly relying on the Father, he will see a gradual improvement. Two seemingly opposing factors are necessary – the will to overcome, and the ability to place oneself in God's hands, devotedly, completely, trustingly. I shall be looking forward to hearing how things are going with Ivan, and I assure you both that I have deeply and unceasingly prayed to the Heavenly Father to inspire strength and guide Ivan according to his receptivity. No matter how thick the dust of ignorance collected through the incarnations, the shining surface of the soul cannot be obscured forever, but must sooner or later be revealed in the blazing light of God. It is up to us, with the help of God and Gurus, to take the necessary steps.

I enjoyed reading your letter to young _____. Please tell him when you write that I have not forgotten him, and convey to him my personal good wishes and blessings. Thank you too for enclosing Leo's letter. I had a letter from him very recently, and I am pleased with his progress in every way. Those who have the devotion and willingness to strive for God will reach Him. Please give him my love again when you write and also send my love and blessings to Ivan. I hope to write to him soon, and will be happy to hear from him at any time he cares to write. Please let me know whenever I can be of help. Please let me know about the taxes with the property. I will write more about the land when I hear from you. Is it a healthy place? Could we develop a colony there?

With all my blessings for your divine thought
Very sincerely

P. Yogananda

P.S. Our colonies are springing up everywhere
P.Y.

Oct. 7, 1949

Dear Ivan,

Thank you for your informative letter written in September.
I have been extremely busy which accounts for this delay in
replying to same.

I am pleased to learn that you are striving to meditate to
the best of your ability every night. Remember never to go
to bed until the peace and joy of His presence permeates the
depths of your soul. God demands 100% loyalty and devotion
from those who yearn for the conscious realization of His
presence. He is not satisfied with only a portion of your
attention and devotion, but waits behind the screen of life
until we consent to give our all to Him. Through steadfast
intent upon the goal, it is finally attained. "Whose heart
is filled with satisfaction by wisdom and realization, and
is changeless, whose senses are conquered, and to whom a
lump of earth, stone, and gold are the same: that Yogi is
called steadfast."

Am glad that you are writing regularly, your idea about
recording the poem, "God, God, God" is an excellent one.
Perhaps it will be possible to do this at some future time.

Be assured of my daily prayers that you may progress physically, mentally and spiritually.

Unceasing blessings,
Very sincerely yours,

P. Yogananda

A BLESSED VISION

I was in Florida as the 1948 Christmas holiday season approached. At Christmastime, I was feeling bad because I could see nothing that seemed to celebrate the true spirit of Christmas. It seemed everywhere I turned, there was nothing but drunken revelry. I went to the beach one night to find a peaceful place to meditate. I was feeling the presence of God as the ocean. Even so, I had apparently been judging those who were not celebrating the true spirit of Christmas. As I looked out in the darkness, a wondrous light appeared out over the water. As it drew closer to me, I saw what looked like the spiritual eye. Then I could see the shape of a person in it. As it came still closer, I could see it was the face and body of Christ! Appearing directly to me, he spoke words of love that were also meant as valuable learning to me. He simply said, "Forgive them, for they know not what they do."

Master was appreciative of the biggest and smallest things that were done for Him. Sometime after the blessing of the vision of Christ, Master wrote to me about it.

A contemporary painting of Jesus Christ

Dear Leo:

Was very pleased to hear from you and to learn of your beautiful experience on the 23rd of Dec., which shows that God hears every Soul-whisper of the devotee, and that he comes when the devotee cries for Him with all the fervor and urgency of his heart.

I cannot tell you what you have done in giving your car to the organization. You have become the instrument of God, fulfilling a great need at the Phoenix Center. It was a most kind gift, given in the true spirit of divine love. I had been trying to locate a second hand car, but up to that time had been unable to do so. Too, the vast expense of supporting the 94 people living here and at Encinitas made it difficult to accomplish at that time.

Everyone was jubilant beyond words to see this demonstration from God, which came through you and your mother. It was publicly announced during the Christmas celebration here on the 25th, when over a hundred and fifty persons were gathered here. I so wished you could have been with us and actually seen the joy of all these divine souls at the demonstration, which came through you. Never has the organization received a car voluntarily donated at such a critical moment. The progress of the work at the Phoenix center was jeopardized because the leader could not travel the vast distances necessary to visit those in need. God bless you for bringing the answer to his problem in Phoenix through God. All my heart's love and thanks. Certainly the blessings of God will be with you for helping to fulfill this need of spreading the work.

Very sincerely yours,
P. Yogananda

P.S. I almost forgot to thank you for the lovely birthday card, which you sent, and for the sentiments expressed therein, which touched me, deeply. My deepest pleasure is in knowing good souls who love God, and in establishing His temple in their hearts. I feel the depth of your love and sincerity, and I pray that you may more and more strive to feel the Divine Presence with you night and day. It is good that you have a little quiet place to go each morning and evening to meditate. Keep up your meditations and the chanting and continue to grow in God.
P.Y.

November 30, 1949

Dear Mr. Cocks:

I was deeply touched by the letter you wrote-it is always my greatest pleasure to help in whatever humble way I can those sincerely seeking Souls who desire to find God. It is only because I have been in seclusion the past several weeks that it was impossible for me to reply to your letter sooner.

When we first hunger a little to know what life is about, we are led to a book, or perhaps a lecture that is helpful to us. As our hunger increases, we may be led to a teacher or given help through friends, and finally, when the hunger is unappeasable, God sends us the Guru, who is the one through whom God speaks to us, the one who remains with us eternally, offering unconditional friendship, until we find God ourselves. That is why I always honor my guru Swami Sri Yukteswarji and all the great gurus of Self-Realization.

Now you must remember the old adage, "when there's a will, there's a way." If you have positively made up your minds that your only desire is to find the Cosmic Beloved, then pray unceasingly to Him to guide you to the right thing you should do in everything. You must not become discouraged by the disadvantages of your environment, but in a cheerful way make the best of it, try to do everything in your power to overcome its worst features, and above all pray to the Father to release you, if that is His will. Even though the others around you are materialistic and sensual, you need not be influenced by them. Seek good company, for as my Guru often said, "Good company is greater than will power." Be quiet and pleasant yourself, and you will influence others instead of being influenced by them. When others are sleeping, you can pretend to be, but inside be awake in God.

You have expressed a desire to become a student worker in the Golden World Colony at Encinitas. If it is God's Will, this will all work out in time. For the present, the Colony is overflowing with students, monks and sisters of the Order, to such an extent that there are no further accommodations available. In time, we hope to extend our facilities so that more can come.

Please keep in touch with me regularly and let me know how your spiritual life is progressing. I will be deeply praying for you, that your desire to enter the spiritual path may be fulfilled, according to His Will. May His Light, which shineth in the darkness of material delusion, though we see

it not, manifest itself to you, and illumine your path home
to his abode in omnipresence.

Unceasing blessings,
Very sincerely yours,

Paramhansa Yogananda

February 14, 1949

Dear Leo:

I was very pleased to hear from you and to learn that you have taken the "Renunciate's Vow" as given in the "Whispers from Eternity." I am always happy to see good souls who love God dedicate their lives to Him in this path of Self-Realization. The Gita says, "Out of one thousand, one seeks Me; and out of a thousand who seek Me, one finds Me – the last shall be the first." Those who last to the end, and never give up heart in their search to find Him, are first to enter Heaven and drink of His bliss. May your devotion to Him ever increase, and may His blessing direct your steps on the spiritual path. I deeply pray that all obstacles may melt away in the blazing fire of your ardor for Him.

You see how much you have gained already, through the teachings, despite the fact that your service in the Navy keeps you far away from here and busy with other things. You have made room for God in your life, and He has responded to your love because of your sincerity and your determination to let nothing stand in your way. That is the way it must always be, for you will find that, no matter where you are, or what you are doing, there will be a thousand things to distract you from your goal, but where there is a will there is a way, as you have already demonstrated. You are right to consider your term in the Navy a test – this whole life is really a test of God – and you will see that when you remain steadfast and sincere, ever devoted and loving to Him, His Will will manifest for you, and He will release you when the time is right, according to His wisdom. I am so happy that you are so deeply following this path, and my prayers and blessings are constantly with you. Please write me regularly, as you have been doing, so that I can be of more help to you in guiding you in your spiritual endeavors.

Unceasing blessings,
Very sincerely yours,

Paramhansa Yogananda

March 2, 1949

Leo E. Cocks, S.O.S.A.
Class 649-A
Fleet Sonar School
Key West, Florida

Dear Mr. Cocks:

Thank you kindly for your remittance of $1.00. We have ap-
plied 50¢ on an SRF button and 50¢ on incense, in accordance
with your wish. This order was shipped to you on February 28.
It is our hope that it will afford you spiritual inspiration.
Please be advised that we do not carry prayer beads or the
Wonder Silence Maker. Some students find that the application
of ear stoppers, as used by swimmers is effective. This can
be purchased in most drug stores.

We trust that you are deriving unceasing good from the
lessons. Should any questions arise please forward them to us
that we may answer in detail, for we are eager to cooperate
with your advancement in every respect.

Continue as you are, devoting your love to the Heavenly
Father that you may serve as a channel for His expression.
Thus will you experience divine happiness–that which lies
beyond all happiness.

To the Master's blessings we add our own best wishes for
your every success in God's name.

Yours in divine fellowship,

Faye Wright

For: SELF-REALIZATION FELLOWSHIP

P.S. Please know that Paramhansaji has blessed a strand of
rudraksha beads (prayer beads) that were made in India of
seeds. He is having us mail this special gift to you from
him – with ceaseless blessings.

March 24, 1949

Dear Leo:

So happy to have your letter dated the 15th of this month,
and to know that the rudraksha beads reached you safely. I am
glad to have you tell me of your spiritual experiences. Your
mother also has told me of some of them, and I was pleased.

Regarding your question concerning my having been a disciple of Sri Ramakrishna - the Yogananda whom you saw mentioned was a different one. It was through the grace of a
great disciple of Ramakrishna's, Master Mahasaya, that I received the beautiful experience of God as the Divine Mother,
but I was not a disciple of his. He told me that I would meet
my guru later, and that my experiences of God in terms of
love and devotion would be translated into the terms of his
fathomless wisdom.

I shall tell you if anything is amiss with your spiritual
development. Please continue to write me regularly, about
once a month is all right, or oftener is you feel inspired
to do so, so that I may guide you more closely through my
prayers. If you will continue to keep in tune with me, and
with Him who sent me, you will be all right. I know you are
faithfully studying your Praecepta and meditating. That is
good.

With love and boundless blessings
Very sincerely yours

Paramhansa Yogananda

THE IRRESISTIBLE FORCE MEETS
THE IMMOVABLE OBJECT

When I got to Florida, I started writing to Master at least every week, sometimes more. Writing to him made him more personal to me. I knew he cared. I'd write about what my activities were, how my meditations were, what was happening etc. He would answer about every other letter. I would get a couple of letters from him every month. If I wrote every week, I'd probably get an answer every two weeks. I asked him if I could become a monk. I told him I wanted to come now. He wrote back and said there was no room. I told him I didn't need a room. I said I could sleep on the floor in the living room or something. He wrote back and said there wasn't any space available. I remember I said: "Well, I'll sleep on the back lawn or the front lawn in a sleeping bag and I'll even bring my own bag." I asked if I could come on weekends. But he kept postponing it. They didn't have any room, no rooms, no bedrooms–nothing–there was no room there. I was told to hold off, but I didn't give up. I guess He was testing my desire and perseverance. That's the way it went for the whole time I was away until December of 1949.

I would try to meditate where I could; the beach at night was one of my favorite places. It wasn't always a good choice though. One night I had set up a tent with my altar pictures, candles and incense. It must have looked strange to the Navy Shore Patrol that passed by. They showed up at my meditation and asked what the heck was going on in there!

March 10, 1949

Mr. Leo E. Cocks, S.O.S.A.
Class 649-A
Fleet Sonar School
Key West, Florida

Dear One:

That was a beautiful letter you wrote me just recently. I have been away from Headquarters quite a bit, and am just now finding a moment to answer. I cannot tell you how happy I am that you are improving and progressing in this path. Yours is the spirit of the true disciple, for in desiring only to fulfill the will of God and the Guru, you are fulfilling the first duty of a disciple. If you continue as you are doing, meditating deeply morning and evening, and holding the peace and joy which you feel in meditation throughout activity as well, you will find increasing response from God and the gurus.

I am very happy to know that you will have the opportunity to receive training along practical lines, according to what you tell me. Electricity, plumbing, carpentry, all these would be extremely valuable to you and to the Fellowship. There is so much construction work to be done, and skill and knowledge would be a tremendous help. I am proud of the way so many of my boys have learned these difficult things through practice and observation, but to have advanced training would be a real asset. Also, it is always good to be able to type and to take shorthand.

In reply to your second question, yes, it is possible for one who is advanced to become a Swami, no matter what his nationality.

God bless you. May you never lose sight of the high goal, which you have set for yourself, and may your efforts find favor in His sight, that by His grace you may attain the ultimate bliss of perfect communion with Him.

Unceasing blessings,
Very sincerely yours,

Paramhansa Yogananda

PARAMHANSA YOGANANDA
Founder

SELF-REALIZATION FELLOWSHIP

PUBLISHERS
Self-Realization Magazine

3880 SAN RAFAEL AVENUE ● MOUNT WASHINGTON ESTATES ● LOS ANGELES 31, CALIF.

April 21, 1949

Dear Leo:

Your sweet letter came to me several days ago, and I was so happy to hear from you again. Please keep on as you are doing, and you will be all right. To have devotion is one of the greatest things in finding God. He is so simple, like a child, and we have only to approach Him as children to win Him. "A humble magnet call, a whisper by the brook; on grassy alter small, there I have my nook." God hides from us only because He is afraid we don't want Him, and He reveals Himself only when He is convinced by the unceasing fervor of our prayers and the depth of our devotion that we really do desire Him above everything.

Your letter to the Philosphical Library was forwarded to me for reply, dear one. I am glad that you are seeking inspiration from spiritual books, but I believe that you will find all you need on the subject of yoga through your study of the Praecepta. Yoga is the science of communing with God. Through the Self-Realization studies and techniques of concentration and meditation you are learning that art. There are many highways and byways of yoga, different paths leading to the same goal. You have already found the main highway, the airplane way; therefore it is best to stick to one good thing than to confuse the mind with too many divergent ideas. I say this, not to restrict you in any way, but to guide you safely on the path you have chosen. Sir Edwin Arnold's translation of the Bhagavad-Gita, known as "The Song Celestial," is excellent, and Thomas a Kempis' "Imitation of Christ" is a wise choice for any devotee who is devoting his life to the service of God and Christ. There are a number of good books concerning the life of St. Francis which you would probably find inspiring, and a fairly recent book called "Five Saints that Moved the World" is very worthwhile. There is an account of St. Francis' life in this, and also the lives of St. Teresa of Avila, St. Ignatius, St. Anthony and St. Augustine. Reading is good if it inspires you to greater efforts for God. Otherwise it easily becomes a useless habit and a waste of time. I never read books - I plunge instead into the infinite sea of wisdom

Leo Cocks   -2-   April 21, 1949

and knowledge, the library of the Infinite.

As you know, I am always glad to hear from you, even though
I cannot always answer promptly. I have your highest welfare at heart, and I will be your friend eternally. You
know how to keep in tune with God and the great gurus, and
if you keep on that beam you will one day discover the eternal radiance of the light of God, and that you are one with
it.

                    With all my love and blessings,

                    Very sincerely yours,

                    P.Yogananda

PY:jcb
Leo Cocks S.A., 1st Lt.'s Div.
Fleet Sonar School
Key West, Florida

P.S. - I forgot to mention the "Yoga Sutras of Patanjali" -
prepared by M. N. Divedi - which is available at the Headquarters. I have just recently completed preparing material
for a book explaining the aphorisms of the great sage Patanjali, but it is hard to say when this will be published. In
the meantime, however, you would probably enjoy studying this
book.

June 7, 1949

SRF - 3060
Leo E. Cocks, S. A.
Flag Division
U.S.S. Albemarle A.V.S.
C/O Fleet Post Office Norfolk, Va.

Dear Mr. Cocks:

Your words echo the devotion that lies within our own hearts, for the wisdom of God's love. Our prayers are indeed with you, and it is our belief that you will attain your dream of service to the Infinite, through the unfoldment of your personal self-realization. Your thoughts and love are directed and dedicated to God, and by following the guidance of the Master, they will not stray from Him.

Your remittance of $10.00 will cover your membership dues through-November 30th of this year. A receipt for this amount is enclosed.

God bless you, Mr. Cocks, and may the light of His presence ever brighten the pathway of your life.

Yours in divine fellowship,

Faye Wright

For: SELF-REALIZATION FELLOWSHIP

2 LEO DETERMINES TO BECOME A MONK

Leo wants more than anything to leave the Navy and take monastic vows in the Self-Realization order. Yogananda postpones admitting him and writes instead of the nature of discipleship, while praising the useful skills Leo is acquiring. Faye Wright, the future nun Sri Daya Mata, writes with encouragement too, while Yogananda encourages Leo's mother, Mrs. Anderson, in her efforts to create a home meditation center in San Jose. Leo visits the US East Coast and meets Yogananda's early disciples, Dr. and Mrs. Lewis and Swami Premananda. A crowd is expected at the Mount Washington ashram for Christmas; Leo is among the visitors and at last is discharged from the Navy and accepted as a monk of the Self-Realization Fellowship.

August 5, 1949

Dear Leo:

Sorry I have not been able to answer your sweet letter sooner, but matters in connection with the work are proceeding
at such a fast and furious pace, I am busy day and night.
I never dreamed Divine Mother would give me such a great
task as the task with which she has just entrusted me, and I
am continuously working these days to bring her plans into
fruition.

Because I am so extremely busy, I am doubly pleased that
you are so willingly and loyally following the path true
to the highest principles of Self-Realization. Through your
attunement, you are not only helping yourself to the greatest degree, but also helping me. I have so many dear souls
to look after, and when they are really in tune then I am
able to work with them through Spirit effortlessly. Divine
Mother knows of your deep desire for Her presence and She
knows every effort you have made, and all your good thoughts,
dear one. So meditate as deeply as you can, as long as you
can, as often as you can and practice the presence of God
all the time. Then you will find sometime when you may least
expect it that the Mother of Universes has taken Her right-
ful throne in your heart forever to remain there, enshrined
by your devotion.

Unceasing blessings,

Very sincerely yours

P. Yogananda

Oct. 5, 1949

Leo E. Cocks
S.A. S-2 Division
Norfolk, Va.

Dear One:

So happy to hear from you - have been wanting to answer for
some time but Divine Mother has kept me busy with so many
things until now. It is wonderful to feel the devotion of
your heart for our Divine Mother, and I know how eagerly
you long to serve her in an even greater capacity. God will
show us the way.

Regarding your question about reservations at Encinitas
during the holiday season, I don't think this arrangement
would be too happy a one for you. As you probably know,
nearly everyone in Encinitas comes to Mt. Washington for the
Christmas meditation and the Christmas banquet. We are so
over crowded now that in recent years it has been necessary
for many to go back to Encinitas Christmas Eve and return
next day or find other accommodations for the night. In the
past it had been possible to close the Hotel, since everyone
was gone, and if so this year, you would find yourselves
quite alone. I will try to find out what arrangements will be
planned this year, and perhaps something can be worked out.

My thoughts and prayers are always with you, dear one and
I hope I shall see you soon. Your mother has indicated there
is a possibility of your getting a discharge within the next
few months. I was so delighted to hear from her that Ivan is
taking hold so wonderfully and responding to the treatment
at the hospital. I was deeply thrilled to see how God is answering our prayers for him. May he continue with the same
faith in the Father, that through his attunement the Father
may send greater floods of His healing vibrations to him.

Your mother tells me _____ is reviving his interest in the
work too. That makes me happy. Please convey my blessing to
him if you are keeping in touch.

Keep me informed about yourself, dear one, and let me know whenever I can be of help to you. I am so happy to give to the Father the devotion and loyalty you have expressed toward me, and I hope that there may be many more souls like you that I present to Him with a bouquet of souls whose sole desire is to be one with Him.

Unceasing blessings,

Very sincerely yours,

P. Yogananda

November 3, 1949

Dear One,

So happy to have your letter dated Oct. 10. Of course you can stay here with the boys if you wish. Most of them will be sleeping on the floor, for we are extremely crowded at the holiday season, but you are surely welcome to join them. They will be glad to welcome a fellow devotee of Divine Mother's. You had better bring your own bedding, by the way, if it is at all possible. Perhaps you have a sleeping bag you could use.

With regard to your good mother and father, I must still refer you to the hotels or motels for accommodations for them. Although I deeply wish that they could stay here at Mt. Washington. Nevertheless I want them to be our guests at the meditation on December 24th, and for the Christmas dinner and subsequent festivities on the 25th as well as yourself and Ivan. If you are not familiar with the hotels of Los Angeles, the Chamber of Commerce would probably be glad to help you with the list.

St. Lynn is indeed still with us ever busy for God and His devotees. However, he spends a great deal of his time in seclusion, immersed in the Divine Joy of God's presence. I am always happy when he can be at Encinitas and we can meditate together. Dear One, the devotion which you so sweetly express I give to our Divine Mother, at whose lotus feet we both worship. May her blessings ever guide and help you on the spiritual path and may Her love reflected in you draw other good souls to this path. "My mother is everywhere." That is a song of Ram Prashad. He sings, "Will that day come to me, Ma, when saying, Mother Dear! Eyes shall flow tears." They are the tears of Divine Joy.

Unceasing blessings and love,

Very sincerely yours,

P. Yogananda

October 5, 1949

Dear Mrs. Anderson:

So nice to hear from you again and I am truly filled with joy to hear of Ivan's steady and encouraging progress. Please give him my deepest love and blessing when you write. I have wanted to write to him again myself, but it seems I have been caught in a veritable deluge of activity, and I have had to put it off. He is never far from my thoughts, and I have prayed for him many times. If he continues to keep in time and strives to overcome, I am sure he will in time succeed.

Regarding Leo's possible release, I deeply pray that it may be affected soon. However, since his release is contingent on your statement that he is needed at home, it would not look well for him to come directly here. Best to go home first - he could perhaps come down for some weekends to see how he lives our way of life and to meditate alone and with the other boys; then he will be better able to decide about making a definite change. His feet are firmly planted on the path, and I am sure God will guide his steps at every turn.

You and Mr. Anderson are working very hard, I see and I am glad you are fixing up your place. It is always good to make things beautiful for God. Am very pleased that you want to have other students in for meditation at your home that it may be a little temple of Self-Realization. That is very good - perhaps a group can be established which can become the nucleus of a center in San Jose. I always encourage students to get together for study of the Precepta and group meditation which each helps to uplift the other. We can discuss it in more detail when I see you during the holidays. I most certainly do want you and Mr. Anderson and Ivan to be our guests for the Christmas meditation on the 24th and for the banquet on the 25th and I am sorrier than I can say that we cannot give you room here - I think Leo will sleep on the floor with the boys, we talked of it in our last correspondence.

The little hotel at the bottom of the hill is called the Marmion Hotel, but I do not know if it would be an acceptable place or not. As I suggested to Leo, the Chamber of Commerce or the Automobile Club could probably give you a list of the names and locations of accredited hotels. I am so glad you can stay over for my birthday too.

Delighted to learn that you visited San Francisco Center and that you have met Kamala and her husband. They are a very fine spiritual couple, and I am sure they are doing much to spread our work in San Francisco.

Your experience was a very beautiful one – no one can say when God will reveal Himself completely to the devotee – He alone must decide. You must continue in devotion, and faith, confident that He will reveal Himself when He deems the time is right. Each glimpse of His veiled presence inspires us with deeper longing – let that longing fire your meditation until the little flame of your devotion will merge in the vast fire of His Bliss.

Unceasing blessings,

Very sincerely yours,

P. Yogananda

P.S.

Very pleased at the news you told me about _____. Be sure to send him my blessings and assure him of my prayers for his highest welfare. We must choose one path and then stick to it. Otherwise we end up in complete confusion. I shall be happy to hear from him at any time if he cares to write. My blessings and love again to Ivan and Leo.

MASTER INTERCEDES TO GET LEO OUT OF THE NAVY

While I was in the Navy writing to Master, I talked to the Navy chaplain (a Catholic priest.) He seemed to appreciate my desire for a monastic life. But then he asked me, "What order are you going to?" So I told him, "It's a yoga order, they believe in Jesus too." "Oh my God," he said. "You'll be going to hell, you're better off in the Navy!"

So that course didn't work out. I kept trying and writing letters. Everybody in the Navy told me normally it takes about two weeks to process these things. (It had already taken about 2 1/2 months.) Master kept asking me how it was coming. I wrote back and said, "It doesn't look good!" From what I had heard, there was no formal notice of rejection. But they don't just give you a discharge. Then Master told me, "I am praying to Divine Mother about your discharge." In the next day or two, the discharge came!

December 2, 1949

Dear One:

Your letter expressing your loyalty and devotion sent sometime ago touched me deeply. I would like to have answered
long before this but have been so extremely busy on some
special work that all my personal correspondence has had
to wait.

I was so very happy to hear that when you visited Swami
Premananda and his boys it was the week-end when Dr. and
Mrs. Lewis were there. They are indeed devoted souls on the
path to greater and greater God-realization through our
Self-Realization Fellowship. Dr. and Mrs. Lewis have helped
me more than words can say to put the Fellowship on a firm
foundation so that all who have been seeking and have found
us can have a spiritual home to come to, in fact many spiritual homes; here on the mountain too, Encinitas by the sea
and the men disciples' retreat in the desert. To read your
loving enthusiastic letters makes me feel that it is all
worthwhile, when I know how much you are looking forward to
being with the boys this Christmastime. I shall look forward
to seeing your parents too.

As you have noticed, Swami Premananda has been working
patiently, intelligently and diligently through the years to
make his church another firm bulwark for SRF in the East. You
have probably heard me say that I prefer a soul to a crowd
but that I like crowds of souls. So gradually in a devoted
way, with God as the goal and with the help of our Gurus SRF
is growing into crowds of souls.

I have prayed that if it is Divine Mother's will you will
get your discharge papers. What is happening? Have you heard
anything since sending in the necessary information? I would
like to hear.

Unceasing blessings will come to you as you meditate at
the Blue Lotus Feet of Our Divine Mother, and what Joy!

Ever sincerely,

P. Yogananda

Leo E. Cocks, S.A.
S-2 Division, U.S.S. Albemarle(AV-5)
c/o F.P.O., Norfolk, Va.

ACCEPTED AS AN SRF MONK

My discharge came towards Christmas in 1949. I still hadn't had any resolution in my desire to become a monk. I went to Mount Washington for the Christmas meditation. That first meditation was a long day, but I had some good meditation periods. I felt good in the Presence there. Durga Ma sang *Divine Love Sorrows*, which was very inspiring.

I don't know if I spoke to Master then or the next day (social Christmas.) I went up to him afterwards and I knelt down to get his blessings. I just was saying within myself (almost like a mantra) "Please, Can I come now? Can I come now?" He looked at me, he concentrated on me and then smiled a little bit. After a minute or two, he closed his eyes for a minute. Then he said, "All right, I changed my mind. You come now." Then he said: "You go see your parents. Visit with them for a few days or however long you want. They haven't seen you for awhile." I was accepted as an SRF monk at Christmas in 1949.

PARAMHANSA YOGANANDA   PUBLISHERS
      Founder   Self-Realization Magazine

SELF-REALIZATION FELLOWSHIP

International Headquarters

3880 SAN RAFAEL AVENUE   ●   LOS ANGELES 31, CALIF.

Dec. 29, 1949

Mr. Leo Cocks
Flag Division
W.S.S. Abermarle (A.V.-5)
%F.P.O. Norfolk, Va.

Dear Leo;

      I wish to thank you for the lovely
Christmas greeting and for your generous
gift to me. It will be used in whatever
way that God dictates.

      May the New Year bring to you the
desire to more and more dedicate your life
to the doing of God's will through constant
tuning in with Him by deeper and deeper
meditation. God bless you, and may the
blessings of the great ones be showered
upon you -- now, and throughout eternity.

                 With unceasing blessings, I am
                 most sincerely yours,

                 P. Yogananda

                 Paramhansa Yogananda

PY/w

3 LEO'S FIRST LESSONS AS AN SRF MONK

Leo absorbs many lessons in conversations with and letters from his guru Yogananda and from Faye Wright. He receives his Initiation into Kriya Yoga and is shown visions by his Master as golden light; but he is disciplined as well. Yogananda shows him the light of the spiritual eye and Leo gets ready to dive in. Then Leo is sent to work with two other monks on the order's goat dairy in Phoenix. He worries that he is being sent to Siberia as punishment. But as the dairy's bookkeeper, he often visits the Mount Washington ashram in Los Angeles and there sees his guru. In Phoenix, he experiments with many austerities, while also learning the hard way that his guru knows everything he and his fellow monks think and say.

FIRST LESSON AS A MONK

When I first set up my room at Mt. Washington, I had two altars. One had all the SRF Gurus and the other had a picture of Ramakrishna and Vivekanada. A few days later Master came into my room. One at a time, he bowed to both altars. He said that he revered Ramakrishna and that he was a great soul. Then he said, "Now you have chosen your path with the SRF line of Gurus, so you need to be faithful to this path. If you aren't wholeheartedly devoted to one path it would be like putting one foot in two boats – you would fall." As soon as Master left, I took down the other altar!

A WELCOME GIFT FROM FAYE WRIGHT (SRI DAYA MATA)

When I got to Mount Washington, I ended up with a nice room. When I first went in, found that it had been fixed up nicely. It even had fancy little curtains and all that stuff. I came in there and I said: "This is not monk's work, they don't do stuff like that." We (the monks) weren't as refined as that. Then I heard afterwards that Faye had been the one who had fixed up my room so nicely. I was very touched by that.

Faye's monastic name is Sri Daya Mata. As I got to know her, the thing that impressed me about her was—work, work, work. She was always happy and smiling. She didn't sit down to eat or anything like that. She made sure that everybody was taken care of—all of the monks and nuns. She would run back in the kitchen and bring stuff out. She was a server, a very selfless soul.

I guess that is why she is what she is - a great soul.

December 18, 1950

Dear Br. Leo:

Thank you for your letter received today. I have given Rev.
Bernard your letter to him, and you should have a word from
him before long.

The little verse which I believe I gave you over the phone
comes from the St. Francis of Assisi, whom Master so dearly
loves:

"Accept criticism, blame, accusation silently, without re-
taliation, even though untrue and unjustified."

What a wealth of trouble and heartache one saves himself
if he but strives to live by this truth! One need not become
a doormat, but by first learning to control himself, to be
the master of his own emotions, he is then freed to speak
with quiet authority and to better serve his Lord and His
children.

Should the foregoing not be the verse I quoted over the
phone, let me know. One suggestion, each day after meditation
take one verse or thought from Master's Whispers or Songs of
the Soul or any of his writings, and strive to live by that
truth throughout the day.

Again, many thanks for your kind words.

In God and Guruji,

Faye

MASTER INITIATES ME INTO KRIYA YOGA

Sometime after I was accepted into the ashram, Master asked if I wanted to get initiated into Kriya Yoga. He gave me a choice saying, "If you want it right away, I'll set it up with another monk and you could get it right away." I said: "No, Sir. I don't want to get it from someone else. I want to get it from You, even if I have to wait." I wanted something like that to be very special and I believe that with Master it would be even more so.

In 1950, the time came for me to receive Kriya from Master. He would bless you and give you the rose petals. When he came to the blessing part, he touched me and it was: "Boom!" It was almost like he knocked me out. It wasn't painful or anything. But I didn't know where I was for a time. Master saw me like that and called an usher. He told the usher: "Help Leo back to his seat." The monk took me by the arm and we walked across the front of the chapel. We walked to the back on the other side (making a loop around the room.) I thanked the monk who helped me and said "I am okay now." The whole experience was a tremendous blessing. It was a spiritual blessing. You do not get things from Master that do not have a purpose—even though you don't know what the purpose is. In many cases, you'll ask him and he won't tell you—sometimes it isn't beneficial to know.

I think that Rajarsi (Janakananda) was there too. He would hold flowers and assist Master. At one of the ceremonies, he went into samadhi and fell on the floor. They took him and put him over by the door for some fresh air. A little while later he came to. He was all right, he just went into samadhi!

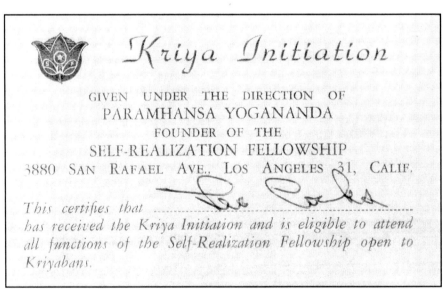

Kriya Initiation

GIVEN UNDER THE DIRECTION OF
PARAMHANSA YOGANANDA
FOUNDER OF THE
SELF-REALIZATION FELLOWSHIP
3880 SAN RAFAEL AVE., LOS ANGELES 31, CALIF.

This certifies that ....
has received the Kriya Initiation and is eligible to attend all functions of the Self-Realization Fellowship open to Kriyabans.

MASTER SHOWS ME THE LIGHT
OF THE SPIRITUAL EYE

After the initiation there was something I had wanted but had never asked for. It was the only time I asked him outright for something. Master was talking about when he blesses you. He said, "The light of God will go through you. Some of you will see it; some of you will feel it. I can show it to anybody." He said that during Kriya, everybody was half bathed in that light. Well, I didn't see it. I felt something but I didn't see it. When we compared notes later, two of the other monks didn't see it either. There was a line of people in front of Master that wanted to be shown the light. The two monks were the last two in line. Taking each one at a time, Master had them kneel down and he put his hand on their spiritual eye. He then said a few things to them, as if guiding their focus and getting them closer to seeing it. Then it was my turn. I said: "Sir, will you show me the light too, please?" He looked at me with surprise because I didn't usually ask for demonstrations. He said: "What! You too?" And I said: "Please?!" He said: "All right." Then He said: "Leo's the last one, the last one!"

So I kneeled down and he said: "Do you see it now?" And I said: "No, Sir." Then he said: "It is over to the left, concentrate so it will be centered." It was like he was looking at the back of my head. I looked where he said and then I could see it. Then he said: "Now, center it. It will get closer and closer." It did get closer as I got it centered. I didn't know if it was either getting closer to me or I was getting closer to it. It was kind of hard to tell. It felt like I was about ready to jump into this beautiful liquid pool!

And then he said: "Do you see it right now?" I said: "Yes, Sir." And then he pulled the plug! At that point I couldn't see it anymore. If you pull the plug from the wall, the lights will go out. That's what I came to understand later on. When I saw it it was like a giant ocean–a singular, strong, whitish sort of light. I didn't see any divisions in it. I didn't look for the blue or any of the other components of the spiritual eye. If they were there I would have probably noticed.

The only time I saw it differently was the experience in Florida when it coalesced into the form of Christ (explained earlier in the book.)

MASTER BECOMES GOLDEN LIGHT

One of the first services after I was accepted, I saw Master at Hollywood (Church). I was concentrating on him. He was talking at the front and then all of a sudden, his body just became this golden light all over. It got brighter and brighter. I closed my eyes and it was still there. It was the same with my eyes opened or closed. There was no more body of Yogananda. It was just the voice in this light. There were several minutes like that. Then the thought came to me (from him), "This is who I really am." Afterwards, the light condensed and the image of his body got stronger. It was like the light got back injected back in the body and he came back to normal. Then it was just like a regular service. I never did speak to him about it or to anyone else. I don't know if anybody else ever saw that or had that individual experience. I never looked for experiences. It almost seemed like a welcoming gift from him.

BREAKING ATTACHMENT TO FOOD USING THE BOWL TECHNIQUE

While we were working on the construction of India house in Hollywood, we were fed by the cook there. I heard about this bowl technique to break attachment to food. You just put it all the food in a bowl and mixed it all together. One of the others would ask, "Are you doing the bowl meal?" And I would say. "Yeah." Then they would say: "You are supposed to put everything in there. You have to put the milk and your ice cream in too." So, I dumped those in with everything else. It kind of spoiled it! I don't know how long I did that. I did it for a while. I was trying to be a good yogi.

SLEEPING ON A ROCK BED

At our Phoenix ashram, we made our beds out of planks of wood – hard wood. Then we added a couple of buckets of rocks on top of that. We put a sheet over it all so it looked okay. (Until you sat on it and then, oh my God!–Maybe I'm not that sleepy yet!) So you didn't go to sleep until you were really tired! You would lie down on the bed and have to wiggle yourself into a position so that you wouldn't feel the rocks. Then you tried hard not to move your position. If you did move or turn, Ouch! You woke up and you had pain! This didn't last forever, thank God! After awhile, we had enough.

This didn't come from Master, somebody had heard about it from the lives of Catholic saints or something. But we were trying to force things ahead, to quicken our spiritual progress. But some of those things could serve to just slow you down!

DAILY ROUTINE AS A MONK

I wasn't at Mount Washington long. While I was at Mt. Washington, we were building India House in Hollywood. We'd get up about five every morning. We would do our energization exercises, and then meditate in the chapel. Then we would eat and get in the car to go work at India House. We would work in the morning and then have our lunch (see the bowl story.) Then we would work in the afternoon and drive back to Mother Center about five o'clock. We would energize, meditate and have dinner. We didn't talk at meals, so during dinner I would read the *Autobiography of a Yogi* again. (You could bring a book in with you during meals as long as you didn't talk.) After dinner, you'd study or do what you wanted to do. It was a pretty set routine, there wasn't much personal time. Sometimes, I would spend some time talking to my closest friend.

HOW TO DEFLATE A PUFFED UP DISCIPLE

There was a time when I was feeling "puffed up" about something (I don't remember now what it was). During this time, a lot of my friends and fellow monks were growing beards. I went to ask Master if I could grow a beard too. He took this opportunity to deflate my ego in two quick sentences: "Not you, Leo. You'd look like a baboon!"

MASTER SENDS ME TO PHOENIX

Master called me in one day and told me he wanted to send me to Phoenix. (There was a church and goat dairy there.) I thought I was being sent to Siberia or something! At first, I thought it was a punishment. I thought I had done something wrong. In fact, I asked him, "Have I displeased you, sir? Have I done something I shouldn't have?" He put a nice twist on it. He said, "No, I'm sending you there to be an example." And he said: "I'll be with you." So I got over the disappointment right away. I knew when I got over to Phoenix that one of the younger monks was having problems. There was a third monk who had been in the order longer than me. He gave pretty good talks. But the younger monk hadn't really had a chance to know Master. When he came in the ashram, he had gone right out to the goat dairy alone. He was able to go see Master in LA once in awhile though. One of the duties I had there was to keep the books for the dairy and the church. So I was able to come over to Mother Center every month to bring the receipts and the bank deposits. I'd bring them to the nuns to straighten everything out. Usually, I would get to see Master too while I was there. It was also a blessing in disguise because I got to know and have more contact with Rajarsi.

MASTER KNOWS I HAVE QUESTIONS, EVEN WHEN I DIDN'T REMEMBER!

Sometimes questions that I wanted to ask Master would come up in my mind when I was in Phoenix. I would write them down. But when I was in his presence, all else was forgotten! It was just nice to get to see

46

him, you know? That was always a great pleasure that way. You didn't have to do anything. You'd just look at him and he kind of made you a little drunk! There was the joy of it, just being there. I used to tell him, "Oh, I am just so happy to be here with you." I didn't have any problems there with him!

He would ask if I had any questions when I was with him. I would say, "No, sir. I am just happy to be with you."

He would say: "Yes, you do. You wrote them down. Next time, bring them with you." So I said: "Ok."

When I got back to Phoenix, I remembered those things. So I wrote them down that time and I stuck them inside my coat pocket that I was going to wear. Then I would get back to Mother Center and be in his presence again. It would be the same thing! He would ask me again. He said: "You have some questions for me."

"Oh." I said, "No Sir, I'm just so happy to be here." He said: "Yes, you do. They're in your pocket."

Then I realized these things he said: "I know everything you think and say." That became a reality to me. It's pretty incredible, that you can meet somebody like that. There are a few of them around. But many of those great souls are in seclusion (in the Himalayas).

This story about the questions was told in the SRF video, *Glimpses of a Life Divine*. It used to surprise me hardly anyone would ever ask me what the questions were. Would you like to know?

1.) I asked "Sir, if I follow you to the end of this life with faith and devotion, will I be able to go to Hiranyaloka with you to see your Master?"(Hiranyaloka is the astral planet that Swami Sri Yukteswar discusses in the *Autobiography of a Yogi*.) I thought I had a good advantage. Sri Yukteswar said he would be on Hiranyaloka.

And since the requirement for being on Hiranyaloka was the attainment of Nirbikalpa Samadhi, I thought my Guru would have to train me or bring me in to get there! And I would also get to be with Sri Yukteswar as well as my Gurudeva!

But the thought occurred I might be totally lost there. On Hiranyaloka, they are creating universes. And I might just be thinking, when are we going to have dinner?! But I thought that Rajarsi will be there and some of these other very saintly people. A lot of the SRF nuns that passed on were pretty great souls too.

2.) I wanted to make sure that I would see my Guru and be reborn with Him in the next life. So I asked: "If I follow you with faith and devotion to the end of this life, will I be able to join you and Babaji in the Himalayas in the next life?

Would you like to know Master's answer to these questions?

To the first question he said: "Yes, you will be there. You will see all the Great Ones. You will be free."

To the second, he said, "Yes, you will be there." So he said Yes to all of them!

But then he added a big (and important) caveat! He said: "*If* you keep on like this to the end."

So this tells me we can't go to sleep at the door. We have to knock and go through the door. To me, this means the use of devotion.

THE GOAT DAIRY IN PHOENIX

One of the monks in Phoenix had an idea to start a goat dairy. The idea was to provide some income to support the church. The monk took the idea to Master. Then he also had to work on Rajarsi to get the money to buy the goats and property. The dairy started with only a few goats, maybe a dozen or so. But some of the goats would go dry and some would have to get pregnant again to produce. You had to try to rotate them around. But that wasn't enough goats to make money. The monk who started it all went out in the valley where a lot of goat farms were going bankrupt. They found a big farm that was selling their goats. They went ahead and rented a big truck and they had something like 120 goats. Another monk and I were there when that truck came in and they all starting coming down the ramp. And they all needed milking!

Milking all those goats, oh man! My arms and fingers were so sore afterwards! But we processed them all and we did get milk. We sold more milk, but then we had surplus milk. The original monk had another idea – "We can make cheese! It keeps longer and we can sell it later." We got some rennet or something like that. We put it in their feed, I think. And we got milk. Then we made these barrels of some kind and made the cheese. But the trouble was it didn't come out right. It was like a big barrel of rubber! You could chew it but you couldn't swallow it! We had all of this cheese in a big icebox and found out that we couldn't eat it. We had to throw it all away. So that was a losing proposition. Since Rajarsi had financed it, I didn't think that he was going to keep throwing money away on something that wasn't working.

When the dairy was finally closed, I was there by myself for a few weeks. I got kind of lonely and finally called Master one night. We talked, I felt better and that was it. A few weeks later it was all sold and I moved back to Mt. Washington. A short time after that, Master was in a car with a bunch of monks. I came up to the car and the first thing Master said to the other monks (about me,) "He calls me at 3 o'clock in the morning, collect!!"

He really had to be more like a mother, because we were very childlike sometimes.

While I was waiting for the dairy to be sold, Master told me, "Do not fail to take advantage of your time there. You will never know what you missed." Looking back, I had some of my best kriya meditations there.

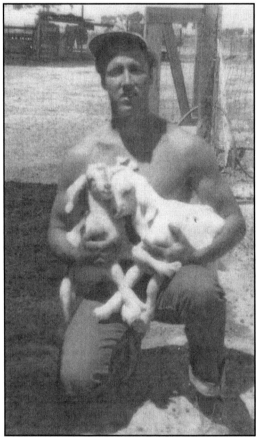

Leo with two of the adorable goat kids

INOCULATING THE GOATS?

The monk that had the original idea to start the goat dairy later thought we should inoculate the goats against disease. I didn't think it was necessary. I could not see how the goats were going to get infected. We cleaned them well and we fed them well. We were separated from everything out there. The nearest place had some cows but there was at least thirty feet between our driveway and an old barbwire fence. Our goats could not go over there and the cows couldn't come over to our place.   So there was no physical contact. But the other monk was more medically oriented and he thought we should inoculate.

I was supposed to be in charge there, so I told the other monk I disagreed with him. We decided we had better ask Rajarsi about it and see what he said. We went to Mt. Washington and he came downstairs to talk with us. Rajarsi closed his eyes in meditation for a minute. Then he said: "You know boys; I don't think you are going to need to inoculate them. I think the goats are going to be alright." I thought: "I gotcha, buddy!" (to the other monk). So we didn't inoculate the goats. In the end, there was never any problem with them.

THE PHONE CALL

After a Thursday evening service in Phoenix, the three of us (monks) went back to the dairy. We had some hot chocolate and for some reason, started talking about our lives before the ashram. We were all talking about if we had any serious relationships before we all became monks. Then the phone rang. I left the others and went into the kitchen where the phone was. I picked it up and all I got to say was "Hello?" It was Master. He said: "Why are you breaking my rules?" He said: "Why are you talking like that?" First I tried to answer Him by saying, "But, but, but, but…." And then I quickly changed that to "Yes, Sir. Yes, Sir!"

After Master was through, I went back to where the other two monks had been. I said: "It was Master. He knows every word you said, and you said and I said. He said we shouldn't be talking like that because we are monks now." So we finished our chocolate in silence!

The three monks of the Goat Dairy (Leo is in the middle.)

Founded in 1920 by
PARAMHANSA YOGANANDA
CABLE: "SELFREAL"

PUBLISHERS
SELF-REALIZATION MAGAZINE
PHONE: CAPITOL 0212

SELF-REALIZATION FELLOWSHIP

3880 SAN RAFAEL AVENUE   MOUNT WASHINGTON ESTATES   LOS ANGELES 65, CALIFORNIA

<u>Disciples at the Goat Dairy</u>

January 17, 1951

Dear Ones:

Just a short message of thanks and appreciation to you all for the many wonderful gifts which you so kindly bestowed upon this self during the Christmas and birthday celebrations. I was deeply touched by your personal messages. At the feet of the Blessed Mother I place each gift as a token of loyalty and devotion from Her children. I never forget you all, so do your part by cooperating wholeheartedly with one another and meditating deeply with ever-increasing devotion. Do not expect everything to work out perfectly. Each of you must be patient and strive to help one another. You are together for a purpose. The devotee must pass all tests before the Divine Mother is convinced of his sincerity and devotion.

I am ever with you -- doubt not and you will realize the truth of these words. Follow the path to the end and you will have no cause to regret your efforts.

With unceasing blessings to all, I am

Very sincerely yours,

P. Yogananda

Paramhansa Yogananda

P.S. Would like very much to have negative of the superimposed photo that the Cocks brothers sent to me. Am very pleased with this gift as well as all others.

July 16, 1950

Dear Leo,

Thank you for your letters sent recently. I have been extremely busy with a dear friend from India along with the editing that has to be done.

One point in your letter I question: I gave Brahmachariship to you at your asking. That means you took a vow for throughout your life. I was surprised to see in your letter that you said if you ever had the slightest thought of leaving, I should bring you back. I want you to know that the highest offense against God is leaving and neither God nor Gurus ask those back who willingly forsake them. Such souls have to go through incarnations before they can again attain their former status. You should let me know what is in the background of your mind. It is due to your deepest devotion that I sent you there as an example. Your devotion must not be like the straw fire, which burns high, but dies quickly! Only on your dependability will rest your salvation, so let me know if you are oscillating and have desire to go away, and why the evil force has been sending these thoughts to you which I never thought would come to you.

Your trouble with ___ or anyone is your fault also. You must learn to get along with everyone even if they argue. Best way is that you do not reply and then there cannot be any argument. Lord Krishna said that "out of one thousand, one seeks Me. Out of the thousand who seek Me, one knows Me." The person who lasts to the end enters Heaven but not those who enter this path first necessarily. Try your utmost to conquer ___ by love. He responds to love more than anger. You must all learn to get along with each other, for though each may have his faults, yet he is the child of God. You should all help each other out with love and understanding and not be stumbling blocks in your struggle to reach your goal.

Regarding ___, it is my policy to give each one fair treatment. Now you must abide by my judgment, which comes from the Divine. I will settle the issue and discuss it when I see you all. In the meantime, I am instructing each of you to say nothing.

I believe it would be best for ___ to receive the Initiation in August and then we can settle everything.

I am very pleased by your tone of devotion in the letters. This devotion for God and Gurus must last to the end and become stronger, thereby enveloping all. I am glad that you are all working toward the development of the work in Phoenix. St. Lynn will stop for a few minutes in Phoenix on Thursday and you can give him all the details regarding the Dairy. Mrs. Coates will give you the exact time of his arrival. I understand that the train will be stopping there for a few minutes.

With unceasing blessings I remain, with all my love,

/s/ P. Yogananda

P.S. Thank you for your kind donation.

July 21, 1950

Very dear Leo,

Your words in your last letter pleased me most - for that's what I told my guru - although others left Him and followed Satan, I always followed my guru. That's why thousands upon thousands are being helped in this path.

I am not interested in those who do not love my Father and Gurus to the end-they are my own who love God and Gurus forever.

I sent you there [Phoenix] for an example. Please don't tell anything about your private life except to me. Never mind temptations, I know all about it - love of God is a greater temptation? Drown everything in it.

I am so happy about your positive attitude [toward others.] That's the only way! I was deeply hurt that even the thought of leaving entered your mind.

Now I am pleased with you [ ] ever. Keep this devotion to the end of life and you will reach God.

Do your best at Phoenix and God will give you victory (over that.) Thanks for the honey dipped prunes (we used to sell it) and dates.

All my love and blessings

Unconditionally given unto you,

P Yogananda

P.S. Divine Mother never chops off the head of true devotee. Who goes to Satan and turn back - they suffer.

PY

LEO GAINS INSIGHT INTO HIS GURU AND HIS DISCIPLES

Leo discusses with Yogananda what it means to be an avatar and observes the complete devotion of the millionaire businessman, Mr. Lynn, now Rajarsi Janakanda. He experiences the generosity and wisdom of Rajarsi, as well as his own mother's devotion. Leo witnesses the presentation of his stepfather's portrait of Yogananda's guru, Swami Sri Yukteswar to his Master. And in his experiences with automobiles, Leo knows the protection—and discipline—of his Master. Leo comes to a fuller understanding that Yogananda knows "Every thought you think," and learns vital lessons in surrender.

IS MASTER AN AVATAR?

I was in Phoenix talking to some members after a service that another minister had given. I was outside and somebody asked me the question, "Is Master an Avatar?" I said: "Well, I've <u>always</u> thought he was an avatar." I felt that from the very first time I laid eyes on him in San Diego. The other minister heard what I said and told me later: "Leo. I don't think you should tell the members Master is an avatar unless you know for sure." He was in charge there, so I said all right and stayed quiet. I didn't say it anymore to anyone else.

Shortly after that, I was on a trip to Mount Washington. While there, they gave me a message that Master wanted me to stop by Twentynine

I BECAME MY HEART

Palms to see him on my way back to Arizona. I got there, he came out and we started walking. He held my arm and he had his little cane with him. He was looking at the little pebbles on the path we walked upon. He'd see a little larger pebble and he would hit it with the cane and knock it off the path. When we were with him, you didn't open the conversation with him. You waited for him to start. So I walked with him and we made a trip or two around the compound—five to ten minutes in silence. He finally said: "What's all of this business about me being an avatar?"

So, I just told him. I told him I felt that way when I first met him in San Diego. I knew he was an avatar. I knew he was my Guru. I told him I knew I had been with him before.

Master said, "Well, I will say this. Whenever a teaching of this magnitude is brought, God always sends it with an avatar."

THE LOVE AND SACRIFICE OF A GURU

One time after the last Kriya ceremony in 1951, I went up to Master's room to see him. It was the first and only time I ever saw him in bed. He had his legs stretched out. There was a chair by the bed and I sat there. Part of the time we were talking–or rather, he was talking and I was listening. Actually, I would think thoughts and he would answer those!

I thought: "What's the problem? What's wrong?"

And he said: "It's my legs." And then he said: "This is because of the last Kriya."

I knew he had taken on the karma of others at the Kriya Initiation. There were so many people at the ceremony that people covered the first floor from the chapel all the way back into the book room and into the foyer.

And I was thinking: "What is it like?" (to have taken all that karma.)

He answered my thought and said: "The pain is like a saw going through my leg. What Jesus suffered on the cross for hours, I've suffered for months in my legs."

58

Then he said, "Divine Mother told me not to give the last Kriya ceremony."

Maybe she realized that all of that extra karma Master had taken would mean a great deal of suffering.

And then Master said: "I know you all wanted it so bad, I decided I would give it anyway."

That's a high state of consciousness! If Divine Mother tells you one thing and you say: "No, I am going to do it this other way." Master's state of consciousness is one with God the Father. To me, Divine Mother was God's consciousness in creation, if I have it right? Master's consciousness transcended from the physical, to the astral, to the causal; to that which is the joy of God the Father (beyond creation).

And I thought one whole leg of Master's must be for my (bad) karma!

AN EXAMPLE OF THE PERFECT RELATIONSHIP

While I was in Master's room talking with him, Rajarsi (Saint Lynn) came in. I'm not sure if he was going back to Kansas City or going to Encinitas. He came in to say goodbye and goodnight to Master.

I thought: "You know, this is very private. I should leave." So I asked: "Sir, do you want me to go in the other room?" (This was in the bedroom and the living room is just a short hallway away.) He said: "No, you stay." So I just stood up towards the end and back of the bed a little bit.

Then Rajarsi came in and he pronamed. Then he touched Master and Master touched him. Then he grabbed Rajarsi and pulled his head down and kissed him on his spiritual eye. Then Rajarsi kissed Master on Master's spiritual eye and then they kissed on the cheek. They talked a little more. The whole sequence was repeated several times.

I'd never seen such affection, such unconditional love in my life.

Interesting, I thought. That's the perfect disciple. (Rajarsi.) And I wanted to be just like him.

Leo's favorite picture of Rajarsi Janakananda (St. Lynn)

A SECRET GIFT FROM RAJARSI THAT FULFILLED A SECRET DESIRE

Rajarsi blessed me on the way out that night; he put one hand on my heart and his other hand in mine. When he did that, I felt something in my hand. I didn't know what it was until he left. I opened up my hand and he had stuck a $20.00 bill there!

At the time, monks were getting $2.00 a month as an allowance–so that was almost a year's income. I knew this was for the amulets I had wanted to place on my kriya beads. The amulets would start with Christ, Krishna, Babaji etc; spaced a dozen beads apart. A total spacing of sixty beads would get me through half my Kriyas. It was just a little personal way of feeling your closeness, oneness and appreciation–the whole works. I wanted to make rings of the Gurus and I had found a jeweler. For $5.00 a ring, he'd put on the little amulet of each one and connect it. Four amulets total–which cost $20.00. But I hadn't mentioned that to anyone–not even Master. And yet, Rajarsi was in tune with Master and he would pick up things like Master would. He knew!

The four amulet rings: Lahiri Mahasaya, Babaji, Yogananda and Sri Yukteswar

RAJARSI JANAKANANDA (SAINT LYNN)

After Saint Lynn had left, Master said, "He is just a great human being. Do you see how great he is?" And I thought to myself: "Yes sir. Oh, yes sir." And Master said: "He's always aware of the power coming from God, through the line of Gurus to Guru and he is always aware of that Divine connection."

He was really incredible, a person with his power, money and knowledge. But he was never seeking any of that for himself. That is the part that Master loved the most. He always did what Master asked. In fact, Master said, "Rajarsi does everything I say, but he doesn't expect the results." If Master asked him to speak in temple, he would. Sometimes he would be a part of our service at Hollywood. One time he came out and stood in the little cove where the podiums were. There was one on each side of the stage. Only one person could stand in there and he gave part of the service there. But normally, he didn't do anything to blow his own horn, so to speak. I never heard him speak about himself or brag about anything he'd ever done or was doing. He'd just do it. He was just happy to be with Master. Sometimes they would get some toys and things. They'd be like two little kids, playing and opening up the toys.

I would always try to get Master's blessings at a social occasion. When Rajarsi was there also, Master would often ask me if I had gotten Rajarsi's blessings yet. I would tell him, "No Sir, I wanted to get yours first." Master would bless me and often he would then say "Well that's fine. You go get his blessing too."

I'd walk over there but he would have fifteen people around him, maybe two or three people deep. I would be three or four people away and I didn't say anything. I just came in and stood there. He would stop talking and he'd open up a little hole and slip through it to reach me. Then he would bless me. And then he'd go back to what he was doing. It only took two minutes and was just a little "day by day" thing. But when Rajarsi would bless me, I could feel Master's presence through him as if it were Master giving the blessing himself.

He had tremendous love, too. It was unconditional love for Master. He was always very attuned to Master in the type of things he was saying. And when he spoke and when Master would ask him to say a few words, you would feel closer to Master. He wasn't bragging for himself to try to get you to tune in with him.

One of the monks left Mt. Washington to go to a Zen monastery. Master said he had been trying to "buy God" with years of meditation and kriya. Master said, "God has disappointed many saints for lifetimes that have had that attitude. You be like St. Lynn. He follows everything I say and doesn't expect the results."

One time after Master's Mahasamadhi, Rajarsi had surgery and couldn't talk. I was walking up the driveway at Mt. Washington and saw Rajarsi walking out the front door at the same time. I figured if I walked at just the right speed, I could meet him directly in front. It worked out just right. Even though he couldn't talk, he blessed me. I could feel Master's presence in him and I could feel that it was Master blessing me through him.

RAJARSI EXPLAINS THE AUM AND MY MOTHER JUMPS IN WITH BOTH FEET!

Rajarsi preferred more to meditate than do anything else, even during social gatherings. When the Mahatma Gandhi World Peace Memorial was being dedicated at Lake Shrine, someone asked where Rajarsi was. One of the monks said to look in a small building that was on the side of the hill above the lake, that he liked to meditate there. Sure enough, there he was. When they asked Rajarsi to come down and join the gathering he did so and sat next to Master. Rajarsi generally sat quietly, apparently in samadhi. Periodically, Master would lean over to Rajarsi and say that he wanted him to meet someone. At that point, Rajarsi would smile and greet the newcomer and then go back to meditating, all the while he apparently was in samadhi.

After the Lake Shrine dedication, Rajarsi was explaining the "Aum" to a group of people gathered around him. My mother and I were in the group. She had never been introduced to him before and she didn't know who he was.

Rajarsi was explaining it and she just popped up and said: "Oh, I can do a much better job than you're doing." I poked her with my elbow to interrupt but that didn't work. Finally, I kind of stomped on her foot. Her feet were tender and then she stopped and asked me: "What are you doing with my feet? That hurt!" I said: "I'm trying to get you to listen to me. You are talking to Rajarsi. He <u>knows</u> God!"

"Ohhh," she said. And she looked so innocent. "Oh, I'm so sorry. I didn't know who you were" she told him as he talked to another person. He just said: "Oh, that's all right. No one can know all of God." You know, it didn't bother him. So that was it and it all ended ok. He went back and kept talking. He was kind of explaining, expanding into spirit. He was getting into and giving to us, that deeper impression into God. It was really good to listen to him. I don't remember exactly what he said now. But, it was nice, you know. Maybe Master had told him to go talk to the people or maybe it was an inner message.

RAJARSI SAVED LEO FROM THE NUMBERS

Rajarsi was so sharp. One time at Mt. Washington, we were talking things over and I had the books for the dairy. There was a long list of numbers with so many dollar signs, etc. I read it to him about three times–so many dollar signs and he was listening. Then I said: "I know the total is $ (thousands of dollars.)" And he just looked and said: "No, that's not right. It should be $xxyx.xx." It was like talking to a computer, he could add it in his head! Of course, he had the right amount. I said: "Oh, I'm sorry, sir." I had transposed a couple of numbers. And I was getting to a point where I could only take so much. But he knew that too and he said: "All right, let's just meditate now for a few minutes and just feel Master here with us." And I just felt "Whew, yes!"

THE FELLOWSHIP ACQUIRES THE LAND ABOVE LAKE SHRINE, WHERE THE TEMPLE AND RETREAT ARE TODAY

I understand Rajarsi was out at the Lake Shrine with Master. I'm not sure just when Master sprung it on him but Master told Rajarsi it would be so nice if we had the land up there, because it has such a nice view of the lake. And Rajarsi said: "We've got views of the lake and the outdoor chapel and the smaller indoor chapel and we really don't need that, you know." So Master just said his thing and dropped it. But Rajarsi picked it up. And I understand that the next day, he went and arranged to buy the land above the lake. At that time the amount paid was a lot of money. It would be in the millions now, that kind of money.

NOTES FROM AN EXPERIENCE WITH RAJARSI IN MARCH 1951

Met Rajarsi coming down the driveway. He blessed me, saying "Gurus grace and blessing be with you." What a tremendous joy and love I felt in my heart. I felt Master's presence so strong that I thought it was Master's physical form that was blessing me. I went in to eat lunch and had to force myself to eat, such was the joy and love I felt. About 15 minutes later Rajarsi was leaving and he blessed me, Henry, Cliff and Andy.

Rajarsi was sitting in the car and as he drove out he pronamed to us several times and he waved to us also. Such sweetness I have never seen before, with the exception of Master. His eyes sparkled with a joy of a little child and the Divine Mother.

Leo (third from left) with Rajarsi (far right) at the Lake Shrine

A YARN PORTRAIT WITH A PROMINENT FUTURE

My step father (Jesse Anderson) was a gifted artist. He made yarn portraits of most of the Gurus. The first one was of Sri Yukteswar. He and my mother brought it to Mother Center to give to Master.

When they brought it into the lobby, Saint Lynn (Rajarsi) happened to be there and came down the stairs. He walked over to them and said hello. He looked at the picture and said, "Master's going to be so happy to see that! Let me take it up to Him now."

So, he took the picture up. (We weren't allowed to go up there like that.) He came down with a lot of compliments from Master. He brought a basket of mangoes from Master along with an envelope with some money in it. There were some notes too. It really did impress him, you know.

Of course, my mother and Jesse ate the mangoes. But as far as I know, she never spent the money. She kept the mango seeds and the money in a pillowcase (or something like that) under her pillow on her bed. She slept with that–I don't know where it finally went. It touched her a great deal too.

As of this writing, this portrait still hangs on the third floor of Mt. Washington. The yarn portraits Mr. Anderson made of Lahiri Mahasaya and Babaji also hang in the building.

Mr. Jesse Anderson with the yarn portrait of Swami Sri Yukteswar

Dec. 23rd

To Mr. Anderson,

It is the grandest picture of Master Swami Sri Yukteswarji-
you belong to the great artist. His picture will have a
prominent place in SRF...Greatest Christmas present. Will send
you both a little gift.

P. Yogananda

To Mrs. Anderson,

Your husband has accomplished a masterpiece in Master's [Sri Yukteswar] picture. It will be an immortal [ ] through the years.

With blessings,

Paramhansa Yogananda

MORE ON THE YARN PORTRAIT
FROM YEARS LATER

April 28, 1965

My Dear Mrs. Anderson:

Thank you so much for the lovely Easter greetings which you sent, and the message contained in it.

We join with you and all of your dear husband's friends and loved ones in wishing him a very blessed 92nd birthday. I remember with so much joy the wonderful yarn paintings that he made of our Gurus, which still continue to hang here in our halls of Mt. Washington Center. I would like Mr. Anderson to know that the picture which he made of Sri Yukteswarji was the very one that Master looked at on the last day of his life, when he stood before it and said, "It is only a matter of hours and I will be gone from this world." We have a great and special love for that particular picture.

Please convey to your dear husband all of our love and special good wishes on the occasion of his birthday.

And, tell him that he is always remembered in our prayers.

God love you both,

Sri Daya Mata

THE RAINS, THE MUD AND MASTER'S GRACE ON SUNSET BOULEVARD

During a winter storm there was a lot of water from the rain. Some of the storm drains backed up and plugged so the water was spilling over the road. It was coming right down the canyon toward the Lake Shrine. It would come right out on the other side of Sunset where our parking lot gate is and shoot right through it. The water started washing the parking lot away. It was pretty bad, with the water rushing down the hill and taking everything with it to the ocean. The monks at the Lake Shrine called and asked me and a couple of the other monks to go out there and help them. We took the truck and filled it with shovels and sacks. I don't remember if we took some sand or not. We had a full load of whatever we could get, trying to go put sandbags there. I was driving down Sunset toward Lake Shrine. The area was pretty well covered over with some trees and it seems to me it was down to two lanes there.

All of the sudden, as we were driving, something turned the steering wheel. I went into the oncoming lane and I couldn't turn the wheel back. I was really trying but nothing happened! Then finally, that wheel kind of let loose and it turned back. As it turned back, I looked back out of the window and where the truck had been turned away; there was no road there anymore! About ten feet of dirt or more had just slid down and covered that whole lane up. If the wheel and the truck hadn't turned, that is where we would have been. The truck would have been stopped and the dirt coming down would have buried us and possibly even turned the truck over in the process. I don't know what was on the other side where the road was missing; maybe it was the canyon or something else. But I have no doubt that Master protected us by making the truck change lanes away from the danger and with no oncoming traffic!

WHERE DO PONTIACS GO?

It was quite awhile before I had any further trouble with vehicles. But this is a story about one of them. I was visiting Mother Center on one of my trips for the Goat Dairy. I was talking with Master in his room before I had to leave to go back to Phoenix. He kept me there quite awhile and it was getting late. Virginia (Ananda Mata) would stick her head in and remind Master that I had a long drive ahead. And every once in awhile, Master would make me promise to pull over and rest if I got sleepy. He did that at least three times and was very emphatic. We finally said goodbye and it was after midnight. After driving the Pontiac for awhile, I felt kind if sleepy and I pulled over to rest. Then I started driving again. Again I got sleepy and again I pulled over for awhile. I got some rest and got a really large cup of coffee.

Starting out again, I drove farther into the morning. I had a determination to get there without stopping again. I started to get sleepy again. I caught myself nodding off and I jerked my head back up. This happened again and once more I jerked my head back up. It happened a third time, but this time I couldn't get my head off my chest – no matter how hard I tried. I felt and heard the car leaving the road and hitting the bushes. But I seemed helpless to do anything about it. The car went off the road and headed into a drainage ditch. It eventually made a sudden stop as it smashed into a concrete culvert. There was a truck driver following me who saw me go off the road. He came running down to see how I was. He was surprised as I was able to kick open my door and crawl out of the Pontiac. He said, "Oh my God, you're still alive!" and he helped me up. I ended up with only a few cuts on my mouth.

One of the worst parts was that now I had to call Master and tell him I had wrecked one of the cars. There weren't many of them in those days. They put him on the phone when I called. "Are you all right?" he asked. I could tell he was really concerned. I told him I was ok but then I had to break the news about the car. Sraddha Mata (Miss Sahly) was in the room with him as we talked. After I broke the news to him about the car, he put his hand partially over the phone and told Sraddha Mata, "Sahly, the Pontiac has gone to heaven!"

Later on, Master could tell that I was still feeling bad about wrecking the car. To make me feel better he said, "Remember, when you came in you gave us a car. So, now we're even."

FROM PHOENIX TO THE LAKE SHRINE DEDICATION ON A WOODEN PLUG

The car we had in Phoenix had a plug on the side of the engine. It blew out just before we had to leave for the Lake Shrine dedication. We had to leave in a very short time and we had to drive all the way to Pacific Palisades–all of us in the same car. We found a wooden plug, hammered it in, and drove from Phoenix to Lake Shrine. I just had a feeling that was the thing to do. It just fit in there and suddenly it got bigger and–you know – what happens to a wooden plug at high pressure? But we got from Phoenix to Lake Shrine with no problems. But I can assure you that there were a lot of prayers while we were driving!

MASTER KNEW ALL YOUR THOUGHTS. EVEN THE ONES IN A CADILLAC

Virginia (Ananda Mata) asked me to clean Master's car. She gave me the keys so I brought it up from the garage and parked it in the driveway where the hoses are. I soaped it, hosed it off and then dried the outside. Then I saw the inside. There were mats in there on the floor and I lifted the mats to look underneath. I guess it must have been a rainy time because it seems like there was some dirt on top of the mats. I did the front mat and then I did the one on the passenger's side. I started to do the one in the back where Master sat. But then I could hear him coming down the hall because his voice was getting louder and louder. So I brushed the dirt on the mat away. There was a fair amount of dirt underneath the original mat. It was covered by another mat and a piece of paper or plastic–whatever they put on them. And I thought: "Oh, that's not that much. He'll never see it. He'll never notice." There were a couple of layers under there so it wasn't obvious.

I saw that he was coming out of the door and heading toward the car. So I thought, "I have to go, I don't want to tie him up." (in other words, delay him.) He got into the car and thanked me. And he said: "You did a nice job. It looks nice." He didn't look under there and see it. They started the car and it just moved a little and then he had them stop! They stopped, he rolled the window down, turned his head and called to me. He said: "Leo, come here." I came over there and he was talking softly, so I stuck my head in the window. When I was close, he said: "Next time, get that little dirt, the dirt down there below my feet." I said: "Yes, Sir." He said, "Otherwise, you did a good job."

A true Guru knows your thoughts! He knows everything you do. You can't hide.

MISBEHAVIOR LED TO A FREE RIDE AND A VALUABLE LESSON

While I was living at the Lake Shrine, I had this desire to ride with Master in his car. You'd see different people with him and you'd kind of wish you could do it too.

Bernard was giving a lecture, a special series, at India House. I wanted to go and I had a ride with a member that was going also. But he wasn't going to Lake Shrine afterwards. He was just going back to Mt. Washington. Reverend Stanley was in charge at the Lake and I told him I wanted to go. He said: "You can't go. You do not have a ride back." I replied, "Yes, I'm going. I'll get a ride. Don't worry about it." Well, I did get a ride but it was only to Mt. Washington. And there wasn't anybody going back to the Lake Shrine.

So I just slept at the Mother Center and then I just started working in the garden there the next day. Master saw me and called me over. He asked: "What are you doing here?" And I told him: "Well, I wanted to see Bernard. I had this ride to his lecture, but not one going back." I told Master what I had said to Stanley: "You know, you are not my Guru–as far as giving me orders."

Master said: "Well, that's true." Then he said, "I thought he (Rev. Stanley) is in charge there." But Master knew that I didn't have a ride back to the Lake Shrine so he said: "All right, get your stuff and I'll take you back."

So, I misbehaved and I got a free ride! I was thinking I would finally get my ride with Master. I would just be there with him and enjoy his presence. So we got in the car and headed for the Lake. I waited for him to bless me and tell me some stories. But he didn't do that. He was looking at a newspaper! Then he would put the paper down and see a car coming. Then he would ask me, "What kind of car is that?" Now when I was a kid, I was pretty interested in cars. I used to go down to the showrooms and see the new models and all of that stuff. I'd tell Master what kind of car it was and then I'd sit quietly again. Then he'd do the same thing!

Another car came and another. It seemed like he did that six, eight, ten times! And finally it came to the point where I realized, "Well, I'm not going to be able to meditate and just be with him like I thought I would. I might just as well relax." I thought I would start to figure out what kind of car it was as it approached. That way, Master wouldn't have wait for the answer. I stopped trying to meditate and started watching the approaching cars. Right at that point, he reached over to me and gently hit my chest with the back of his hand. I felt a wonderful peace and joy fill my chest. From then on, he didn't ask any more about the cars. And for maybe twenty or thirty minutes; I was quiet too, just feeling his presence. I just wanted to do whatever he wanted me to do.

In the end, he gave me what I had wanted. But I had to do it on his terms, you know!

This experience was an important lesson in surrender. I had to let go of my desire to just sit quietly alone with him. I had to tune in with him and what he needed me to do. I had to learn the lesson he was teaching me.

THE POWER OF ONE KRIYA

Master took a drive most evenings. One night after the drive, He showed us how to do Kriya after he got out of the car. He told us: "You should do your Kriya with great intensity. All it takes is one Kriya to get out of the body." And then his eyes went glassy and he was gone! For a minute or two, he didn't breathe. He was standing there for a couple of minutes and then he let the air come back in. Then he took a breath and said: "That is how you should do your Kriya. One Kriya should be enough." That is how a Master does Kriya!

WHAT IT MEANS TO BE A MASTER

One day, Master was lecturing me on life force (specifically, sex energy) control. He was walking back and forth in front of me, punctuating his point about the need to control that energy. He said, "You have to be like a boxer, punching the punching bag of self control!" As he said this, I thought (but didn't say out loud), "That's easy for you, you are an avatar." The second that thought went out, Master answered it. He whirled on his heels toward me and said very forcefully, "And how do you think I did that? Do you think I don't feel that force within me? It is like a mighty river flowing up my spine. BUT I AM IN COMPLETE CONTROL!"

THE MASTER'S ROBE

I was in Twentynine Palms with Master at his retreat there. He came out on the patio when it was almost dark. Then it got dark and started getting chilly. We were standing there and he was talking to us. My knees started shaking a little bit and so did my hands. I couldn't help it and I couldn't stop it. He said: "Leo, you're cold." I said: "Yes, Sir. A little bit, but it's no problem. It's not bothering me." And he told Virginia (Ananda Mata) to get his robe from inside and she brought it out. And then he called me over to him and put the robe on me! As soon as he put it on me, Virginia was walking back in. Just then I had a thought: "I just might forget to bring it back in the morning. Boy, what a souvenir." As soon as I had that thought, Virginia stopped. She turned around, she looked at me and she said: "Leo, now you don't forget to bring that back!"

She was pretty advanced too.

It felt great to have that robe on. I couldn't sleep that night, hardly at all. There was so much love. It was like he was embracing you. I'd meditate in the house, in the chairs, on the edge of the bed. And then I went outside and I walked a little. Then I would meditate sitting in the sand and it was really a good feeling, you know. I did sleep some but I didn't mind not sleeping. It was like the love was embracing you and also energizing you some, too.

I was feeling very special. I even started thinking I had been with him in his past lives like when he was William the Conqueror—I was one of his captains or something. I was thinking my knee problems were some battle injury from past lives with him. My head was getting bigger and bigger—I was so special (because he had given me his robe to wear).

Later, I saw him with about six to eight other monks. He said, "Come here, Leo." I walked up to him and he put his hands on both my knees. I was thinking "What is he going to tell me? Maybe how great I was in battle and who I was?"

He said, "You had too much sex in your past life."

Man, my bubble was really burst (and in front of a lot of other people too). I found out later I wasn't the only one to have that experience. He just knew where to push the buttons!

5 LEO'S GURU SHOWS OMNIPRESENCE, DISCIPLINE AND LOVE

Yogananda acknowledges helping to prevent a Russian-Japanese War. He accepts a prodigal back into the fold, and shows Leo more examples of self-control and protectiveness. To Leo's surprise, the Master also makes him a minister of SRF and gives him the experience of seeing a soul with the three worlds—physical, astral, and causal—floating within him. When Leo falters in his understanding, his Master forgives his misunderstandings and sets him straight, just weeks before he leaves the body.

MASTER USES A "TWEAK" TO HELP PREVENT MORE WAR

One night Master was talking to a few monks and householders after an evening service. They were all behind the Encinitas hermitage on the lawn. At that time, the dictator of Russia was Joseph Stalin. He was interested in attacking Japan. He got on the train in Moscow and was going across Russia toward the seaports closest to Japan. I guess he was going to attack Japan through their back door. But when he had left Moscow and got a little ways out, he had what felt like a heart attack. They stopped the train and took him back to Moscow. They couldn't find anything wrong but they cancelled the trip. This stopped that war from getting any bigger.

Master told those present in Encinitas that night that he had kind of "tweaked" Stalin's heart so that they would had to take him back to Moscow. But it wasn't a permanent thing. It was just a temporary thing to send him back and stop him from broadening out that war. It is amazing how the Great Ones can feel things like that.

A RIDE WITH OMNISCIENCE, DISCIPLINE AND LOVE

Master was loading up to go out to the desert for a few weeks. Divine Mother was pushing him to get his writing done so the books could be finished. He had two vehicles going out there, his car and a pickup truck. Quite a few nuns were making this trip with Master and they were to travel together in the car. He had things well organized, but there wasn't enough room in the car for all the nuns. There was one too many. He wanted me to drive the pickup truck loaded with supplies. So he put Dorothy (Taylor) with me in the pickup because she was the oldest nun. (The idea being that there would be less attraction than with any of the other ones.)

So we headed out to the desert. I knew the rules (monks and nuns weren't supposed to talk to each other, regardless of their age). But I had some serious questions about Kriya Yoga and meditation. I thought that since my questions were about spiritual stuff, it would be OK to ask Dorothy a few of them. After maybe half an hour of driving, I broke the silence and asked her if it would be alright if I discussed a few questions about Kriya and meditation. She said: "OK Leo, that is alright." So I had her permission. We talked about ten or fifteen minutes (really not too much on a three hour drive.) Well, Master was plugged in to what was going on. While Dorothy and I talked in the truck, Master simultaneously repeated our conversation in his car! He started by saying, "Oh, Leo is breaking the rules." Master then described (for everyone in the car with him) exactly what I was saying and what Dorothy was saying in reply.

When we got to the desert, Master was there already and was sitting in the back seat of his car. The back door was open. As I walked by, Master told me to get into the back seat and close the door. I thought "Oh, oh. What did I do now?" After I sat down in the back seat next to Him, Master started to really let me have it. He had never done anything like it before. Master asked me why I had talked to Dorothy even when I knew I shouldn't have. Master had said before: "I know every thought you think." This experience showed Master knew <u>everything</u> about me. Even the little and deepest things that you never tell anybody else, not even the person you are closest to. It was like a scalpel, cutting sharply through the layers of my consciousness. It was so painful that tears started going down my cheeks. Master went on and on. It was so painful that I couldn't take it any more. Without even really thinking about it, I had to get away. I reached for the door handle to leave. Just as I did that, Master put his arm around my shoulder and pulled my head toward his heart. After awhile, Master told me that he didn't say those things to hurt me. He told me that he said them out of love. He wanted to help me change some of the things I needed to change. Then he told me to take the rest of the day off. He told me to meditate and think about all of the things that he had said.

"I know every thought you think." He sure does even if he's not there, doesn't he? That sticks in you mind. And you should be careful in the future about breaking rules!

KARMA YOGA: SELFLESS ACTIVITY

Master had a special love for Jerry, because he was like a lost sheep. He worked by himself most of the time. Jerry had his own car and tools.He was gay and could do almost anything. He did repair work, electrical work and recording work on the record players. He even worked on stuff during the night at his home. He was a real karma yogi and worked really long hours for Master.

He worked at the church and stuff like that. At Twentynine Palms, Jerry put in a new bathroom and septic tank. You have to dig a big hole and then hook up things to it. I worked with him while he was digging. I was up above and I dropped a bucket with a rope down to him. He would fill it up with dirt and then I'd crank it back up and throw it out. But this one time, I was cranking it and–I don't know what happened– somehow it slipped out of my hand when I got near the top. And the bucket just went "Bam!" and it whacked him in the head. I did that twice to Jerry, poor guy! I did it there and at the India House when we were pouring the walls.

In that case, I had a ladder and we got some boards to walk on like scaffolding. I had this board–twelve or sixteen feet long. The other side still had the nails in it. I couldn't get it to go where I needed as I was holding the board. I thought I had hold of it, but it popped out and swung out of my grip. Jerry was walking by and the side with the nails hit him in the forehead. He was really bleeding! The foreman helping us saw it and wanted to run Jerry to the hospital. But Jerry said: "No, no, no. I'm alright." He just put his hand on his head and chanted "Aum, Aum." The blood was just running down his face. I don't think the foreman ever saw anybody like us! In fact I later heard he said to one of us, "I thought you were all going to kill yourselves by the time we got this place done!"

A PRETTY GOOD DEAL!

Master had asked Jerry to meditate. He reminded him fairly often. When Master asked him to meditate with the boys (the other monks), Jerry would say: "I'm can't, I am too busy." He said, "I don't have the time for all of that stuff."

And Master said: "OK, you work for me and I'll meditate for you."

That's not a bad deal!

But that only lasted a few months and then Master tried to tell him– "No, you have to meditate too, now."

A lot of times, when we would go out for our exercises and meditation; we'd still see Jerry working. He wasn't lazy, that is for sure! He ended up in the room across the hall from me. This was a big benefit because one of the jobs he had been given was to convert the old wire recordings of Master's voice to the (then) newer tape. He would do this in the evening when I was around and I got to hear many of Master's original lectures as he recorded them onto the new tapes. I would ask him to keep his door open as he made the new recordings. When he closed the door, I would knock on it and ask if he was going to record that night. He usually would keep it open for me. He was a nice guy and I worked with him a lot as you can tell from the other stories. He really loved Master and gave everything to him.

HOW TO MAKE A HEADACHE GO AWAY

There was one time when Jerry had a headache. He knew Master was there so he went up to see him. When he got up there, (outside of Master's rooms) they told him that Master was very busy. But Jerry was used to being able to see Master when he wanted. He said, "He is my Guru!"and walked right in to where Master was. Master saw him and as he almost always did with Jerry said, "Come on in." Master put his hand on Jerry's head, blessed him and the headache went away immediately.

Some of the other guys heard about this and tried the same thing. They went to Master the same way. But they didn't get the same result and he didn't do the same thing for them. He told them to do the energization exercises or something else. I heard he told one monk to try an aspirin!

He treated Jerry differently. I wouldn't say he was a favorite but Master gave him a lot of things he wouldn't to the ordinary person.

THE MAGNETIC QUALITY OF DEVOTION

James was the first minister in Phoenix (he was also gay). He had a strong love for Master. In fact, the first time he saw Master (in Encinitas,) Master was surprised. He asked James, "What are you doing here,

James? You weren't supposed to come in this life." But the love he had for Master was such a magnetic force it drew him back.

Master needed somewhere where he could work without people calling him all the time. Most of us didn't know where Master's place was in the desert for awhile. One time, James drove from Phoenix to find it. He didn't know where it was and nobody gave him directions to it. But he found the house without an address or directions. When he pulled up at Master's place, Master saw him and said, "What are you doing here? How did you find me?!" James replied, "Divine Mother led me, sir." Master replied, "She would never do that!" (Leo laughed at the memory of this as he told it.)

But James had this devotion that had a magnetic quality. Sometimes when he gave services, the love and devotion that he had for Master would hit you so strongly, the tears would stream down my face. He left later on and I lost touch with him. Years later, I found out how to contact him. In fact, Marcelle and I went to visit him when he was getting close to dying from bone cancer. Even though that is very painful, we didn't see that pain reflected in him. He told me he was ready to go and you could see that sweetness that he had was still there.

A BIG LESSON IN ATTUNEMENT

When Master came back to Mount Washington after being out, he would come through the kitchen at Mt. Washington. One night I really wanted to see Master. So I pulled a small kitchen table over near the elevator and waited for Him. It got late, so I finally lay down on the table and fell asleep. Master came in about 11:30 p.m. and was in his wheel chair, being pushed by one of the nuns. He woke me up by playfully poking me in the stomach with his cane. He said, "Wake up, wake up. I'm home now." Then he said, "Leo, you take me up to my room." The nun who was with Master (Ananda Mata) said, "I can take you up sir, that's o.k." But Master said, "No, I want Leo to take me up." I thought this was great because that elevator was small and I knew there was only room for two people. I could have Master all to myself. I wheeled him down the hall toward his rooms. He was looking at the yarn portrait of Sri Yukteswar, so I stopped. Whenever Master pronamed to Sri Yukteswar his face got softer and gentler, just like a child.

He pronamed to his Guru and I did too.

Then I made a big, big mistake. I asked, "Sir, how tall was Sri Yukteswar?"

Oh! He looked at me with fire in his eyes and he said: "You should never ask a question like that!"

The problem was I was just seeing Sri Yukteswar in only a body form, limiting him to only that.

And a lot of people are like that, you know. They ask these kinds of questions about Master. I've heard that a lot of times. How tall was he? What color was his hair? What color were his eyes?

I have just answered them by saying that I never concentrated on that–that I really can't give them a good answer. And then I try to just cut the conversation off. Because that's not the kind of things he would want us to talk about.

He wanted us to think only about the spiritual nature. As a disciple to your Guru, you don't identify with those kind of things. If you only see the physical characteristics, you can't have much attunement. I don't want to waste my time just trying to satisfy that kind of stuff. Anytime I asked Master that kind of stuff as a disciple, he would shut me down right away.

I learned a big lesson there. You see Him as a Guru, the Divine Guru, the Divine Voice of God, You don't look for all of that pettiness, the physical characteristics. He is so much more than that. If you bring him down to that level, you are missing the boat.

MASTER TAUGHT ME ABOUT MORE THAN TABASCO SAUCE

Master wanted to know what we had to eat down in the monk's kitchen. It was like a little buffet and when mealtime came, you'd bring your stuff down from the big kitchen. When Master came down, it wasn't mealtime. So we had something to set the table with but we didn't have any food. We only had dry cereal there at that moment. We didn't even have any milk or anything, only Tabasco sauce. He took some cereal and just sprinkled the Tabasco sauce on it all over. So much so, that the cereal was almost floating with that stuff. And then, he started eating all of it, cereal, Tabasco and all.

So then, I thought, "I want to be like Master too." (You know, I was young–I was only in my early twenties.)

So I got some cereal and poured some Tabasco on it. Not as much as he did though. Then I put some in my mouth. Then I yelled: "WHAAAAAAAAAAAAOOOOO!" And I ran over to get some water to drink.

Master said: "Look at Leo. He is all burning up inside!"

I didn't have the control he did!

I don't know what he was teaching me. Maybe he was teaching me about Tabasco sauce–I never took any more after that!

But this shows what power these Masters have–power over common things of the world also.

MASTER SAVES ME IN THIN AIR

I was helping paint Mother Center and we were using scaffolding to reach the upper levels of the building. The boards that we were walking on extended about 5 feet beyond the end of the scaffolding supports. I think that I was mentally chanting "Aum Guru" the whole time that I was painting. As I painted, moving across the board, I wasn't paying attention; I moved beyond the scaffolding support and toward the end of the board, causing the board to flip up and me to start falling. I grabbed for the building but there wasn't anything to grab onto. But then, miraculously, the board reversed course and flipped back up into position. It was Master saving me.

A NOTE OF THANKS WITH NO NOTE

We drove the construction foreman nuts, mostly due to our inexperience. He wasn't exactly a follower of Master's, but he had his own experiences that were like wake-up calls. One Christmas, he bought a present for Master. He had it all wrapped up but was too embarrassed to give it to Master. So he put it by the front door of Mt. Washington after hours. There was no note or card with it and he drove off without anyone else knowing. The next day, Master saw him at India house. Master really surprised him when he told him how thoughtful it was to leave a gift and how much he appreciated it!

A SURPRISE FROM "CHARACTER AND KARMA"

I was walking outside at Mt. Washington one day when Master approached me. The first thing he said was: "Kneel down." So I knelt down in front of him. Then he blessed me and said, "I ordain you a minister of Self-Realization, by character and karma." I was surprised!

Sometime later, I was giving my first service as a minister. I was thinking about what a good service I was going to give. I opened with a prayer and meditation. Then, when I got up to give the talk, nothing came out! This went on for awhile. Then the only thing I could think of to say was, "Let us meditate for a few more minutes." But I wasn't meditating as much as I was praying – hard! I knew that my attitude hadn't been right so I told Master I was sorry. I asked him to help me out of this situation. Later, I was told that the talk had been really good. And to this day, I have no idea what came out of my mouth!

"THE THREE WORLDS ARE FLOATING IN ME LIKE BUBBLES"

I was with some other monks, working out at Master's retreat in the desert. He was different there (his state of consciousness was incredible – even more than normal). He would often come a few times during the day to check on us and talk a little. I was working outside on the pool one day and noticed Master coming outside. I called the others to let them know. He came out his back door in a profile (side) view to me. I was the first one there to see him. He was wearing a white shirt with a sombrero on his head. My first thought was, "Oh, he looks so cute." I pronamed as he approached. But then he turned to face me and my eyes met his. His eyes were on fire! There was such power coming out of his eyes that it scared me and I took a few steps backward. I had never seen him like that. Before that experience, it was always this kind of embracing love. He picked up my thoughts and said, "When I look within, the three worlds are floating in me like bubbles."

That is beyond everything. I mean that is a pure Avatar; with the three worlds–the physical, astral and causal–floating in him. That is more than Divine Mother (in creation). He still recognizes the manifested world and is with Divine Mother for a lot of things. But, at least in my mind, he was pure spirit in a bodily form.

February 20, 1952

Dearest and Most-Loving Master:

You said when I was out to the desert, several weeks ago, that I could go to San Jose for a visit for a couple of weeks. At that time, however, my leaving would have delayed Mr. Rogers with his painting; so I stayed until the painting was done. Mrs. Brush's house has all the plastering done but the finish coat, and Henry says that he doesn't need any help putting on this coat. I am leaving this afternoon, and I only hope you don't destroy me for doing this. I know you have the power to do this for you have told me, "All I have to do is think one thought and your life would be smashed". All I ask is that you have mercy on me, please.

I know there is an underlying reason for this visit, and I know and feel that you know this too, but I see no other way to get this problem out of my mind. If I had listened to your words implicitly this could have been avoided, I know. When I come back, I am going to follow your words exactly, to the best of my ability, for by trying to reason out your advice it proved fatal and opened the door for Satan.

You told me in the beginning that you hoped I would always feel free to come to you with my problems; I am trying to be "above-board" and frank with you. First of all, you made me a minister and Brahmachari, which I have never thought I deserved, but more than once I have been referred to as a "draft-board" minister, and this hurts me very much, for I volunteered for the Navy and served 1 ½ years, and I would rather join the service again then hide under the false robe of a minister, for it is true I have no spiritual duties or church to minister in. I do not want to preach but I would like to be able to serve this great work in a more spiritual way, then just laboring in the construction of buildings.

Also you told me at the desert that you wanted me to drive, and now I have been taken me off the driving list, with the exception that I can drive the pickup on the Mt. Washington grounds. I would prefer not to drive at all then to drive under such mistrust.

I have always wanted to please you, above everything else, but instead of feeling that great love that I used to feel in your presence, I feel a fear of you, for you have showed me the Divine Lion in you and it scares me to an extent. I was always drawn to you because of your great love, and I beheld you as a divine kitten and an all-forgiving mother.

You treated me like a true mother, but now I am slightly afraid because I know the stern father-side of you and I no longer feel that motherly-love towards her child. I do not mean that I have not received your help that you have been sending me, for I feel that I have improved much over my former ways, thanks to your grace.

Will you accept me back at Mt. Washington in a couple of weeks? I pray that you will let me come back, again. I will wait until I receive your permission before I return.

With All My Love, Forever,

B. Leo

P.S. Please forgive once again, dear Gurudeva.

February 20, 1952

Dear Leo:

I am glad that you are having the opportunity to visit your parents as I had promised you. While there remember to follow your regular daily routine of exercise and meditation - meditate a lot with your mother.

I am glad that you have written to me frankly, for then I can help you to have a better understanding. Most of your conclusions were unfounded. You have the wrong slant of things. You must learn to interpret everything in the right light.

I have through God saved lives, not destroyed them. I did not come on earth to do destructive work - you have misunderstood my words and me. Every saint is made of thunder and flower. But in regard to principles, one must be stern; one has to be firm in order to carry on an organization.

There are many ministers who have no churches in which to preach - even I have no church of my own in which to lecture. The principle thing about a minister is that he must have control over his senses, think that all kinds of work is for God, and by example help others to follow the spiritual path, and when necessary, work in any field. You are not ready for a minister's position. You have been made a Brahmachari, which denotes a period of training and discipline. You yourself know that you are not ready to preach. When the time comes that you are, I will call upon you. There are many unsettled things in you which must be settled. Preaching is the least qualification of a minister. The exemplary life itself is the preaching. Reform thyself and you have reformed thousands by your example.

You won't be happy until you can learn to really keep your face turned toward Divine Mother - it doesn't matter what kind of work you are doing, as long as you have the thought of Divine Mother with you all the time. Whether you are doing Her work of building, laboring, etc. or of teaching others is the same with Her as long as your heart is right; one is no more important than the other to Her. A devotee's whole concern must be centered around Divine Mother and willing to accept whatever duty is put before him.

I am still the same forgiving person that I have always been. I love you with the same divine love as I have always. I do not change. When you change for the bad, then you are

afraid of me. When you are good, then you see the Divine
Mother's love which is always constant there.

Please give your parents my deepest blessings and divine
love. I was happy to receive a letter from your mother the
other day – and she has probably received mine in the meantime. I am glad that Ivan is listening to my words and I am
writing to him to remain at the hospital longer than two
months, if need be.

When your two week's visit is finished, then you can return
home to Mt. Washington.

God ever bless you.

Very sincerely yours,

Paramhansa Yogananda

[handwritten addition:] with all my blessings that you understand the truth and facts in all situations and not misunderstand. The patient should follow the spiritual doctor's
prescription. I never would do anything except what the
wisdom of my guru guided me to do. Do not be guided by the
mortal habit guided will but by the wisdom guided will of
the gurus. By acting for God and the gurus, meditating on God
and renouncing Ego – misguided desires – the soul becomes
free from bondage. PY

Feb. 23, 1952
Sat. Morning

Dearest and Most-Precious Guruji,

I don't know what to say to you, for you have always been kind and forgiving to me. All I can ask for is your forgiveness, once more. I am sorry that I left the way I did, for I realize, now, that I shouldn't have gone without your blessing. Will you please let me come back again, please. I haven't broken any of the vows except obedience, because I have not mixed with opposites or gone to movies and such. I have been staying at home (my parents' home that is) and studying, resting, and meditating. I feel I have learned my lesson and worked out the desire to come to San Jose now, for I see everything is empty. And I now see what a blessed privilege it is to live at Mt. Washington, my real home, and what a great spiritual light I was living in. While I was in that light I didn't see or appreciate it, but now that I am away I can see how great the light is.

Will you please let me come to see you for a day at the desert and let me offer you my gratitude and little flowers of love and devotion?

With All My Love, Forever and Always,

Leo

MASTER POSED FOR A PICTURE AND AVOIDED THE FLASH

I had a desire to take a picture of Master. I asked if he would pose for me and he said that he would. But he also said: "I'll let you know." I was ready right then. I had a camera with me. Well, I carried that camera around for three months while I was working, waiting for him to invite me to take his picture. Then I finally gave up and left it back in the cottage. I realized I would just have to wait until he asked me.

Shortly after that, he came down to the chapel for a talk with all of us monks. He also had Mrinalini Mata and Meera Mata (her mother) with him. And then he asked: "Is Leo here?" I was over in one corner and I said: "Yes Sir, I am here." He said: "Get your camera out. I'll pose for you now." I said: "Just a minute, sir. I'll run over to the cottage and get it right away." I ran there and got it as fast as I could. I was hoping he wouldn't change his mind before I returned.

When I got back to the chapel, he was sitting in the front row of seats. I positioned myself in front of him. As I was getting ready to focus, He said: "Wait a minute; I don't like the flash in my eyes. I am going to get out of the body first." As I looked at him his eyes were normal. Then, all of a sudden; they turned glassy as he withdrew the energy from the body. Then he said: "Alright, you can take your picture now." Now, at that time, I remembered that the blinking reflex is automatic. It doesn't matter how much you tried not to blink; if there is a flash, it just happens. So when I took the pictures, I was careful to watch his eyelids to see if they closed when the flash came. They did not! He had left the body, but kept the organ of speech open somehow.

You know, he could control the senses that way. When he was with Christ doing his interpretations in the desert, he kept the organ of speech open here on this plane. Most of the time when you go out of the body, everything is dead to you here. But he had absolute control. He didn't have to go through any fancy rituals or anything like that.

The disciple has to learn to resolve themselves to doing thongs the Guru's way. You can't force anything.

The photo, taken with Leo's camera, of Paramahansa Yogananda in Samadhi.

YOGANANDA PROTECTS, BUT KNOWS HIS TIME IS SHORT

Leo observes his Master protecting his disciples, attempting to help his brother Ivan, taking on the karma of others. Brother Herbert also reveals his love and affection for their Master and Leo. Yogananda blesses prayer beads and makes gifts to Leo, while frequently saying that his remaining time on Earth is short.

YOU CARRY MY BODY, I'LL CARRY YOUR SOULS

The day that India Hall was opened, Master sent word that Norman (Paulsen) and I were to wait for him there. The opening was to be right after church. He had us wait for him by the side door coming out of the kitchen–that little parking lot they had there. Master got there about ten minutes to twelve and church was over at twelve. Church was going to let out in a couple of minutes.

There was another usher there and Master called him over. Bernard was giving the service and Master said to the usher, "You go tell Bernard to keep talking until I tell him to quit." Master then turned to Norman and I and said, "You boys help Me downstairs." His legs were still affected from taking on the karma from the last Kriya Initiation.

And I asked Norm, how do we do this? So we criss-crossed our arms into what I think is called a "hospital carry." We held our arms for him and Master sat down. We lifted him up under his arms. He held his arms around our necks and shoulders. We carried him up those stairs and walked across where the people would eat out there in the dining area. Then we took him down the steps that come out behind the stage and the altar. For two people to cross there, it is fairly tight. When we were done, He gave us nice little hugs and said, "That's my boys!"

Then he said: "You carry my body and I'll carry your souls."

And I thought: "Wow, what a deal. I'll take that deal anytime and forever!"

AN UNUSUAL MEDITATION CAVE

Sometimes when someone left the ashram, they would still come by to see Master. One of the reasons that I thought I had been sent to Phoenix was because Master knew that two of my closest friends were going to be leaving the ashram while I was away. It's easier that way, you know—when someone close leaves and they are about your own age. You care for them and you kind of hurt when they go. Norman used to still come to see Master, but he used to come up late at night. We would normally go to bed by ten. He might come by eleven so no one would see him. He didn't want people to see him because of what it would look like. There is a beautiful story about Norman and Master that took place at Master's service. I'll tell that one later.

Anyway, then Norman came up with tools and things and we built a cave on the side of the hill. You come up the driveway there of the main building at Mother Center and then if you keep going, you go back down the hill. (They've put another ashram there now.)

We dug a cave in the hill with an entranceway. It was about ten feet in (with a door), three or four feet deep and then we had boards that were covered over with dirt to make it quiet. Then we went in and dug out a larger room and we dug a shelf all the way around. Norman brought lumber in and we coated it with tar and laid that for a ceiling. We also had an air vent that stuck up through there.

It was quite a thing! But the worst part of it was–there was a lot of poison oak around there! I caught poison oak all the time. Even after we had it done, I'd catch poison oak!

But it was nice. It was real quiet and dark. A few of us used to go pretty regularly for a while. Now of course, it's all buried under a nun's ashram.

THE FULL PROTECTION OF THE GURU

My friend Daniel had been in the ashram for a while and was at Mt. Washington one afternoon while Master was in Twentynine Palms. He had decided to leave the ashram but Master wasn't there to say "Goodbye." Master picked up everything that was going on in Daniel's mind. He told Virginia, "Get the car out. We're going back to Mt. Washington. Now! We're in a hurry! Can you drive fast?"

Meanwhile, at Mt. Washington, Daniel was on his way out. One of the other monks there talked to him for almost two hours. Then, after saying goodbye to the other monk, Daniel was walking out the back door. Master drove in just as Daniel was leaving!

Master took Daniel inside and evidently talked to him so he wouldn't leave. He did stay for awhile. But then he went into the (military) service.

Master loved Daniel very much. There were tears in Master's eyes when Daniel left. But he loved all of us. Daniel was a young man growing up there and he was still in high school. He was working in the print department with the big presses. He was productive too.

After Daniel enlisted, he was sent to Korea during the war there. He had left the ashram but Master's protection was obviously still there. There were two things that happened in Korea that showed this:

He was in a tank that was shelled. The guy who steers and runs the motor is in the lower part of the tank. Daniel was in the upper part of the tank and his feet were on the lower guy's shoulders. Daniel could see outside and so he would press one leg to have the lower guy steer right and the other leg to have him go left, etc. The shell pierced the armor plating of the tank, and the lower soldier was killed instantly. Daniel was OK.

The other time was one night when Daniel was sleeping in a sleeping bag in the combat zone. They used to get out and make a (hopefully) safe spot to sleep. An enemy soldier came on to the line where they were sleeping and killed Daniel's friend with a knife while he was sleeping next to him.

There were a few of those things happening and Daniel was protected that way.

Master said (during the war there) that he was over in Korea a lot.

MASTER TRIED TO HELP MY BROTHER IVAN

My brother had some heavy karmic tendencies that were obvious even as a child. Master tried his best to help him. Ivan was on the path kind of loosely but came down and stayed at Mt. Washington for a little bit. Then Master let him come out to Phoenix to the goat dairy for a little while. He stayed there but he was very restless. He just got too restless. He had to move and go on. He couldn't stay too long in that kind of life (as a monk).

Later, I saw Brother Bhaktananda, he knew my brother too. He said: "Well, if your brother keeps on the way he seems to be going now, in his next life, when he is reborn, he'll be free of that karmic burden. He'll have a normal life."

You know that's about as good as you can get. Earlier, my mother had told me about something disturbing that had happened with Ivan at her home. I was upset when I heard about it. I went to Master (in kind of an accusatory way) and said, "Sir, you told me you were going to help my brother." I related what had happened with my brother and mother. Master replied, "You have no idea how much I've helped him already. You know Leo, even Jesus Christ cannot heal everybody. I could change your brother but I would have to have him with me on a daily basis. And I don't have that kind of time anymore."

In a way, that kind of shows some limitations even though an avatar has that consciousness. It is not always up to them. It can take some time to make changes that become a part of you -- time until they have kind of "rooted," so to speak.

Master kept saying things like he didn't have that kind of time but somehow it didn't hit your mind that he was talking about leaving.

March 22, 1949

Dear Mrs. Anderson,

Please forgive me this long delay in answering your letter of several weeks ago. As Mrs. Miller has probably already talked to you since her visit here, I will only speak briefly here concerning your predicament over your son Ivan.

It is very hard for me to tell you what I did when you wrote before, but my suggestion was based on what appeared to me to be the best plan in view of the facts of the case presented to me. I have a very great love for all people, and I would not willingly hurt anyone. However it is true that we often hurt ourselves, in our ignorance of what God has intended for us, and thus bring much suffering to ourselves.

You may be assured of my deep and continued prayers for Ivan. I can do that much, but in the final analysis, it is he who must help himself - the sooner he can bring himself to realize this and act, the better. For you, I deeply pray too, that in God you may find the courage and strength to help Ivan, insofar as God wills you should.

I have always loved the Divine Mother aspect of God, because Her love is unconditional and forgiving always. It was the same Divine Mother who sternly took my beloved earthly mother from me -- that I might find Her smiling at me from every speck of space. We must break the bonds of earthly limitations by our bursting desire for God. Then all things are possible.

Am so happy to learn of Leo's continued good progress in his spiritual endeavors. He writes to me quite regularly - in fact, I believe my secretary mentioned another letter from him this morning, although I have not yet had the opportunity to read my mail.

I shall be interested to hear how the treatments are working for Ivan. Please let me know how he is getting along. It is true that spiritual endeavors are easier in a healthy body. I was also glad to hear of Ivan's dream. If he accepts my advice that I have given him through you, he may be sure that I will act only for his own highest good. I have no other reason to advise anyone, and you know that I do not correct or discipline anyone unless that person asks me and gives his consent. That was the way I found it when I went to my Master's Hermitage. You cannot imagine what verbal punishment I endured! But I saw that I changed for the better, and beneath the iron will of his discipline, I felt the warmth of his unconditional love.

So do not be discouraged. God's help is ever at hand. Love him and churn the ether with your prayers that you may be guided to the right thing you should do in everything.

With deepest good wishes for yourself, Mr. Anderson and Ivan,

I remain,

Very sincerely yours,

Paramhansa Yogananda

MASTER'S NOTE TO IVAN, FOUND WITH MRS. ANDERSON'S LETTER

It is after leaving a city of electricity for homesteading away from this convenience that one fully appreciates the light – usually it is just taken for granted. And so it is with the spiritual path – one may be too close to the light to fully comprehend its importance in one's life until one has turned his back on it.

If you turn more and more to Her, you will find that your difficulties are but trivial and you will wonder how you could have thought otherwise. The only way out is through Divine Mother!

MASTER HEALED LEO'S FELLOW MONK AND FRIEND HERBERT

When I was first at Mt. Washington, my friend Herbert was in trouble. He was seeing an orthopedic doctor and a neurologist. He was on crutches at the time.

Master asked him: "What do the doctors tell you about your legs?"

And Herbert answered, "Well, it's bad and they want to amputate my legs."

Master just said, "Do you think God could heal you?"

Herbert had a lot of faith in Master. He said: "I think God, through You; could heal me."

Master said: "Alright. Don't go back" (to the Doctors).

Herbert got better and better and better. The crutches went and he was able to sit cross-legged until the day he died. After he left the order, he was doing work he liked with young people at S.R.F. His wife was a psychologist, so they had a license and could treat disturbed kids. They would sometimes bring them in to their home. They did good work and had some good results.

Years later, I talked to Herbert for the last time on a Valentine's Day. He passed away two days later while meditating at lunch time.

Dear Leo,

It was very good to see you at the Lake Shrine and later at Mount Washington.

Am so glad that you are happy in your new cottage on the hill. It is a very secluded little nook. And it would take hardly any imagination at all to visualize yourself in some isolated Himalayan cave deeply practicing divine union with God. The pictures of Master, the Great gurus and St. Lynn are very wonderful and must be a constant inspiration.

Isn't Stanley fine? His organizational ability and his ambitious spirit are really commendable. There is much to be learned from him that will be of utmost value in furthering the work.

We were very blessed to be with Master for a short time. He spoke so inspiringly about the work. Now we are spreading all over Europe and the East. This work will sweep the world and we are so privileged to be with Master. His divine example will spur us ever onward, churning the ether with our yearning for God-communion and giving of ourselves in service to all mankind. I was thrilled with his divine message of magnetic strength and powerful achievement. This is the teaching that will harmonize all religions and bring peace to earth.

I always like to remember the story of St. Francis and will pass it along so perhaps you may benefit from it. St. Francis would appear often in the middle of the town square and in churches but as often as he was found in public preaching about God; just as often he could be found in this cave or that mountain top or this hidden forest on his knees in prayer in fervent adoration of God. He would never speak until his heart was filled with the love of God. Then he would rise and the love, which inflamed his heart, would flow out in the form of divine words and whole villages would be converted. That is the way I feel Master wants us to go. Prepare well yes, but forget philosophy teaching and all and plunge into divine yearning; then after being filled with the presence of God speak from that spirit. Those are Master's words and I am passing them on.

When you asked me if I would answer you if you wrote to me I was so deeply touched. Beloved brother, it would be a privilege to correspond with you and to exchange spiritual messages.

My deepest and heartfelt love to you,

Your brother Herbert

MASTER AND LEO AT THE WISHING WELL

Master was sitting by the wishing well at Mount Washington in his chair. I knelt down and touched his feet. I was kneeling there by him and he asked me: "Is there something I can do for you?"

You know, I would have never asked him for these things. I have always been happy just to be near him and accept whatever he gives me. But when the Guru asks you, it is different.

So I asked: "Sir, would you bless my prayer beads?" They were around my neck. He reached for them and took them off me. I thought he was just going to give them a simple blessing. But he put them around his neck, gathering them together as they hung down. Taking them off his neck, he stretched them out in a line and held each end in both hands. Then with the beads stretched out, he brought them up and touched them to his spiritual eye, back and forth, several times. As he passed them through his spiritual eye, he deeply invoked the blessings of all the SRF gurus. He said each name out loud, over and over: Jesus Christ, Babaji, Krishna, Lahiri Mahasaya, and Sri Yukteswarji. He did this several times, blessing the whole string of beads. He had a way of doing something that would really knock you out. He wasn't just saying the blessings, but blessing them with his whole heart and soul.

I thanked him profusely. But then he asked me: "Is there something else I can do for you?"

I knew that he knew my every thought. I would never have asked for these things because I always felt it was asking a little too much. But since he knew my thoughts and was asking me, I felt it was OK. His asking me changed everything.

I asked Him: "Sir, could I have a little piece of your hair?"

Virginia (Ananda Mata) was there and he kind of yelled over to her. He said: "Virginia, you go in and get me a pair of scissors." She came out with the scissors and he took some hair here and snipped some off. I forget how many, but he cut a nice little bunch there of the ends of his hair.

I realized these were tremendous blessings. But it was because he asked. I didn't (and wouldn't) ask him.

The strand of beads blessed by an avatar (amulets were added later.)

I AM OK TO DRIVE

I had been on a driving restriction. That meant I could only drive on the grounds. Master needed to go some where and for some reason there was no one to drive him. I was aware of this so I asked if he wanted me to drive him to where he needed to go. He replied, "Come here. Come here." He was quiet for awhile and then said. "That karma is all gone now. Everything is all right. You can go back to driving, everything is OK." I proceeded to drive without an accident for the next 50 years.

He knows the karma and the right thing to do for all these things that can come up. We don't know all the things we are being protected from.

There was a monk who came to Master once and asked a question I could never understand, "Sir, what if I ever disagree with what you tell me?"

How could you have that thought? Those things are not agreeable or disagreeable. They are the truth whether you like it or not. Master didn't make up stories. If he told you something, it was the truth – like God speaking directly to you. There is no room for disagreement, even if you don't like what he says.

LEO HOLDS VIGIL AFTER MASTER LEAVES THE BODY

Leo again hears hints that his Master will soon leave the body, but the truth does not register with him. When he learns that Paramahansa Yogananda has died after a talk at the Biltmore Hotel in Los Angeles, he feels relieved he was not there. He holds vigil over the body, which he recalls shed a tear. Long after the Master's Mahasamadhi, Leo feels his presence and help. He still corresponds with disciples such as Doctor Lewis and Faye Wright. He also recalls examples of his own complete attunement with his guru and his God.

THE NIGHT BEFORE MASTER'S MAHASAMADHI

In March 1952, Master had been in the desert. He came back to Mother Center because Ambassador Sen (from India) was here and touring around the different S.R.F. ashrams. On March 6th, I saw Master and talked with him. He had been saying things for awhile like he didn't have much time anymore. Somehow it didn't hit your mind that he was talking about himself leaving. The night before Master's Mahasamadhi he said to us, "I wish that I could give you all the samadhi that I feel." In my enthusiasm I responded, "Give it to me, give it to me!" Master replied, "If I were to give you the divine experience it would incinerate you with a million volts of electricity." I didn't care! I just thought "Burn me, burn me, burn me. Just do it!" Well, I'm here to tell the story so obviously he didn't do it!

Just days before he died, Yogananda and SRF welcomed India's Ambassador Sen. In this photo, Leo stands just behind his Master's left shoulder, between Yogananda and the Ambassador.

THE MAHASAMADHI OF THE GURU

On March 6th Master said to me: "Wish me luck. Tomorrow is a big night for me!"

And I thought, what is he talking about? It's not a big night for him, it is a big night for them! He will be telling them stories and interpreting God-realized truth for them.

I wanted to go to the banquet too. And I asked Master if I could go to the Biltmore on March 7th. I told Master that I had saved the money to go.

But he said: "No, I don't want you to go."

At first it kind of hurt my feelings. But later when I knew what happened, I realized it was for the best. It saved me from going through all that happened there that night. It was painful to think of him going and would have been pretty hard to endure. What can you do?

Later that night in the monk's ashram, someone came over and told us. We were sleeping and they turned on the light and made an announcement. I don't remember who it was.

They brought Master's body back to Mt. Washington that night. We took four-hour shifts watching over Master's body.

During one of my shifts, I had a desire to touch Master as I was standing watch at his feet.

I touched his toes. They were still soft and Master's skin was smooth—just the same as when he was living in that body.

Earlier on my shift, a woman had come into Master's room and expressed her grief. When she left, I noticed that Master had a tear in his eye.

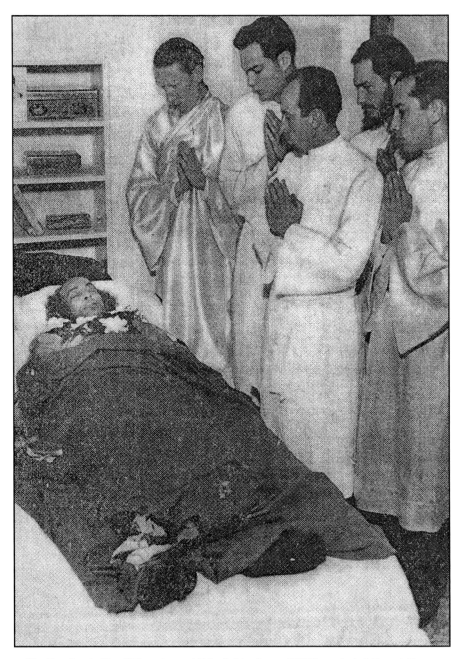

The *Los Angeles Herald Examiner* published this photo of SRF monks holding vigil over their Master after his Mahasamadhi.

A STRONGER PRESENCE

Nobody really knew for sure yet whether Master was going to come back in the body or not. Many times before, He had gone into samadhi and left the body. It wasn't totally clear that Master wasn't coming back until Rajarsi came to Mount Washington. Rajarsi arrived and he went into meditation up there with Master in his room. In a short time, he made contact with Master and asked if he was coming back into the body. Master said he was not coming back. Well, there was nothing Dr. Lewis, Daya Ma or anybody could do. So when they said that was it, we had no reason to doubt it.

Masters funeral was a couple of days later. Rajarsi seemed to take the lead part of it. Oliver Black was there and, of course, Dr. Lewis and all of us monks and nuns. It was beautiful.

After Master's funeral service was over, Norman and I came out the front door and onto the patio. I looked over to the side of the driveway and I saw Rajarsi. I said: "Hey Norman, there's Rajarsi. Let's go get his blessing."

He blessed us. Then he gave Norman a big hug. I was surprised; I had never seen him hug anybody. He hugged Norman and then held him some more. He whispered to Norman and I was close enough to hear it: He said, "You know, Norman; Master loves you very much." That was really heartwarming!

Oliver Black was feeling a lot of joy and laughing. One of the nuns didn't understand and reprimanded him.

I didn't really have a feeling of sadness afterwards. It seemed like you felt Master's Presence even stronger. I didn't feel abandoned or anything like that. He was on a higher plane and still helping us. I felt he was gone but still with us, like he had promised. In particular, when he passed it was like he was trying to make us stand on our own feet.

While I was in Phoenix in 1950, Master told me, "I have given you my unconditional love. Do not fail to take advantage of it, for you will never know what you missed."

Dear Faye,

Just a note to say that my room is in the final stages of completion. I painted it a pastel green instead of the light blue. It looks very nice.

I also wish to thank you again for your many kindly aids in fixing the room. I really didn't expect or want to fix it up so elaborate, but I sincerely appreciate your help. But above all, I am grateful and humbly indebted to you for giving me the push over the wall of a big test that was holding me back from all the progress and happiness. Ever since last Tuesday I have been feeling very joyous and happy inside, just like I used to feel when Master was near me. Now I know beyond a doubt that Divine Mother and Master spoke to me through you and that it is not just my imagination, because I am able to hang on to that feeling, through all circumstances, to a great extent. Please don't misunderstand me, I don't mean to imply that I have a great state, but I know that this is the beginning of that just consciousness.

Thank you again

In God and Gurus,

Leo

P.S. Would you put my parents on your prayer list? Also, if you ever see me or hear me doing anything that you think Master wouldn't approve of I sincerely wish you would tell me. You know his ways much better than I do, so I would appreciate this very much.

May 27, 1952

Dear Brahmachari Leo:

Your letters are very much appreciated. I am only happy if anything I may say to you or my brother or sister disciples draws you closer to the love of the Divine Mother and our Beloved Gurudev.

Throughout every experience we have, we must never lose sight of our goal – oneness with Divine Mother. Master often quoted Christ, "If thy hand prevent thee, cut it off..." If any thought, emotion or habit prevents us from feeling the contact of Divine Mother, we must destroy it by the roots and turn our attention with greater determination than ever upon the Beloved Mother.

May God and Guru be with you, Br. Leo, in your efforts. If you keep on this way to the end of life, God will surely be with you.

Faye

A LETTER FROM LEO'S MOTHER AND THE MASTER'S RESPONSE SHOW THE DEPTH OF HIS LOVE

Beloved Sister Dayamata,

A few lines that I should have written you long ago. To quote a line from a letter from Master written in August of 1949:

"Dear Mrs. Anderson,

Thank you for your two recent letters, which so clearly reflect that wonderful love and devotion for God, which I have always seen in you."
  This line from master is one of my spiritual jewels, which I have hidden deep within my heart and soul.
  On Master's last birthday in 1952, as I knelt before him to receive his blessing, I begged him with tears running down my cheeks, to touch my heart and soul-so that I would feel the Divine Love that he and Rajarsi felt. I told him that my heart had been crying for Divine Love ever since I first heard of it in 1918, when I first began studying Christian Science. It was the only thing in life that I ever wanted or cared about. I told him most women cared about jewels, birds, wealth, position and husbands who would grant them these things. I told him that I only longed for Divine Love. He said to me, "But Mrs. Anderson, you have that love in your heart now." I replied, "But I am not aware of it. Of what use is a gold mine in my backyard if I am not aware of it and still feel poverty-stricken?" The master clasped my hands and said to me lovingly, "By the end of this incarnation, you will realize this love!" as he and Rajarsi exchanged loving glances.
  I have been longing for love ever since and knew Master's words would come to pass. The most wonderful part was that I deeply felt God and Master's spirit everywhere at convocation and in all present there. But I have felt it most deeply in my own heart and soul. God and Master did awaken this spirit in my heart. My heart and soul were like the words in Master's chant: "My heart's aflame, my soul's on fire." It is such a divine, wonderful feeling like being in love, perpetually. I don't mean that this condition is with me every moment; it comes and goes. Sometimes it is very intense so that I have to drop whatever I am doing and go

quickly to my front room—my sacred spot— and sit quietly and
let the Spirit flow over and through me. When it leaves me,
I feel denuded and I cry out, "Dear Lord, what have I done,
said or thought that you left have left me."

Bless you, dear Daya Mata,

In Master's love,

Alice Anderson

Founded in 1920 by
PARAMHANSA YOGANANDA
CABLE: "SELFREAL"

PUBLISHERS
SELF-REALIZATION MAGAZINE
PHONE: CAPITOL 0212

SELF-REALIZATION FELLOWSHIP

3880 SAN RAFAEL AVENUE — MOUNT WASHINGTON ESTATES — LOS ANGELES 65, CALIFORNIA

February, 14, 1952

Dear Ones:

I am deeply grateful to you for the gifts you bestowed upon me during the holy Christmas season and also for my birthday. Please again accept my sincere appreciation for your thoughtfulness. Your sweet thoughts which accompanied the gifts were of special significance to me.

Each day reunite your consciousness with God by meditating regularly with ever-increasing devotion. He cannot escape the net of our love -- the only thing He does not have unless we freely give it to Him. Life has no real meaning without God, so seek Him first, last, and always, until He is yours forever.

May His loving presence permeate your consciousness now and in every day of this New Year 1952, and always.

Unceasing blessings,

P. Yogananda

Paramhansa Yogananda

Mr. and Mrs. J. S. Anderson
101 North 15th Street
San Jose 12, California

P.S. I am so glad you are following my advice. [illegible]

P.Y.

Yogananda's handwritten postscript to his letter to the Andersons says: "I am so glad Ivan followed my advice. So glad you are understanding and ever willing to improve. Wherever Ivan is, God is with him. I am happy to receive your kind letter. My love and blessings to you, your husband and Ivan, sent without measure. P.Y."

MASTER KNOWS I WILL LEAVE THE ASHRAM

Toward the end of Master's life, I worked in the ashram answering Precepta (SRF lesson) questions from students. I wanted to know how I was doing. Master said that I was doing fine. Later though, I was taken off this duty and put in the garden to work. Master told Daya Mata that a time would come in the future when I would leave the ashram. He told her that it would be "my time to go" and to not try to talk me into staying. Daya Ma talked to my mother and told her not to discourage me from leaving the ashram when I had decided to leave.

DOCTOR LEWIS AND LEO
REMAIN FRIENDS

Dear Leo, — I forgot to tell you that I received my pictures from you — I understand that your brother does the work. They are very fine and I am happy to have them. Will you kindly let me know what I owe and I will gladly pay you.

We had nice meditations didn't we — also good discussions

Blessings

Dr. Lewis

THE SWEETEST THING MASTER EVER SAID TO ME

The main part of the path for me is devotion. It seems to me the easiest path to follow that I am drawn to. There are many memories I have of my Guru that bring powerful thoughts of love and devotion. Sometimes Master would touch your hand. A lot of times he would touch your forearm when he walked and sometimes he'd take you by the hand.

And, of course, we'd always touch his feet.

When he touched you, he was healing you without you asking for it. And it was actually his physical hand. When he touched you, there was happiness and joyousness! Desires were gone. Because it was him, what else do you need?

One of the happiest times was when we were at Twentynine Palms. He had me out there a couple of weeks before I was sent to Phoenix. I was to work in the garden on the patio outside his door.

One day, he came out and I got up and walked over to him. I pronamed and I touched his feet. He stood up and took me by the hand. He didn't do that too often–hold my hand. And when he'd do that, I would just close my eyes and feel that contact point; I'd feel the life-energy, his love and all of the Divine things that were flowing into me from him.

I was feeling so much love and devotion for Master. We walked in silence. Mentally taking the dust of his feet, I was telling him I loved him inside my mind. Without words, I kept silently pouring out my love to him, "I love you, Master. I love you, Master."

This went on for awhile. Master knew what was in my mind and heart. After a few minutes, he stopped walking and turned toward me. Then he said: "When you are like this Leo, I can take you by the hand and take you right to God."

This experience was also a lesson for me. I understood that if we approach God and Guru with that kind of love and surrender, it allows us to tune into him. It is there that he can help us the most and draw us quickly back to God.

Epilogue: Leo Re-commits to his Guru and to Living in Spirit

As Yogananda had predicted earlier to Faye (Daya Mata), Leo leaves the SRF Monastic order. He plans to go to India when he saves enough money, but gets caught by the "wave of life" in the world. He is distracted from the Ocean of Spirit and his line of Gurus for more than twenty years. As he reawakens to the promise of the spiritual life, old desires and worldy habits fall away. He feels his Guru taking him by the hand and leading him back to the spiritual path, never to stay away again.

Dec. 22, 1976

Beloved Dayamata,

Just a short letter to tell you how much Master and the Great Gurus have been helping me this last year. For the last twenty or so years, I have been playing with the wave of life, and to a great extent, forgetting the Ocean of Spirit and our Gurus who are manifestations of that Ocean.

This last year desires, worldly interests and many habits I thought I would never be able to conquer have been falling away like old clothes being discarded. I know beyond any doubt that it is Master and the Great Gurus working. On the human plane, I have been especially helped by Brother Anandamoy, who has been very helpful in his advice and loving counsel to a former monk of Master's. In Anandamoy, I beheld such a deep joy and devotion to Master that it literally lifted me to great heights of devotion also. Brothers Sadananda and Ahbedananda have also been very kind, loving and encouraging to me. I know this is Master taking me by the hand and leading back to the path and his work again.

Master promised me many wonderful things if I stayed loyal and devoted to Him and to the path to the end, so I am renewing my loyalty and love to Master, the Great Gurus, and to you, Mother. Please pray for me that my efforts will be blessed with steadfastness and worthiness for the many blessings that I have been receiving.

Most of my worldly responsibilities are coming to an end. Looking out for my Mother is a blessing to me. Her loyalty and devotion have been an inspiration.

To the best of my ability, I am trying to live the spirit of my vows that I took with Master many years ago. I give you my consent to advise, discipline or give to me any instruction you feel Master would want me to have.

The fourth Sunday of the month, I take Mother to the Los Gatos Center and the other Sundays, I attend the Richmond Temple.

I have tried to open my heart to you, even as I would to Master and I know you see my feeling and sincerity.

In Master and Guru's love,

Leo Cocks

A HOUSEHOLDER DISCIPLE IN THE WORLD

And so Leo did the best he could to live in the world as a householder disciple. He met and married Marcelle in 1977. She was no ordinary woman. Her spiritual strength and attunement with Yogananda provided a stable foundation for Leo to live in the world. The photo below shows Leo and Marcelle on their wedding day with Brother Anandamoy.

Leo and Marcelle with Brother Turiyananda on their wedding day

Leo and Marcelle played their roles in the world like most souls do, working at their jobs and going about their lives. Leo's job was physically demanding, but he was able to persevere and earn a retirement.

He attended SRF services and events with Marcelle as the years passed. Those who knew of Leo's time with Yogananda were always eager to hear his stories and he would share them informally with others. It wasn't unusual at the annual SRF convocation to find Leo surrounded by a circle of devotees, eager to hear the inspiring tales.

Leo and Marcelle (her back to the camera) with their old friend
Brother Anandamoy at the 1993 SRF Convocation.

THE POWER OF CONNECTION
WITH FRIENDS

October 20, 1986

Dear Friends,

After almost a year, I went again to see the Lake Shrine, and I found it as beautiful as ever. I was there quite a few years as minister in charge and I always appreciated the wonderful devotees who used to come to the services. My sadhana started practically there, because it was there that I had first met Ma (at that time still Miss Faye Wright) and Ananda Mata. Although I had corresponded with Ma before, it was at the Lake Shrine that I got "caught" in the web of Master's divine love and compassion, exuding from and through her.

And it was at the Lake Shrine that I had also experienced for the first time the reality of Master's presence, when I was meditating on the little bench on the landing before the houseboat. I suddenly lost the awareness of time and space, and was flooded with an inexpressible wave of joy, love and peace. Later I asked Br. Adolf what was so "strange" with that place, and he told me that Master was at one time sitting there in samadhi for a long time. It was similar to what I have experienced long before in Jerusalem, when I was sitting in Gethsemane(then I thought myself an "atheist"!), and was unexpectedly lost in a strange "cloud" of unearthly peace. Then I was just puzzled, and could not understand it, but now I know that it must have been the awareness of Christ's presence, that could not have been erased through the millennia by the hundreds of thousands of restless tourists, and the greedy vendors of "souvenirs". Master once said that the "vibrations" of an avatar remain there for thousands of years, and if one is – by some miracle! – in tune, he may perceive and feel them. The same can be felt and experienced in Encinitas, where Master and Rajasi used to meditate in their high state of consciousness. Unfortunately, we are usually caught too much in our work or problems to be able to tune ourselves into their "wave-length"...

It was so nice to see you both after all this time, and to "excavate" good old memories of the times past! When I look back over all these years, it seems like yesterday when I first came, and hauled rocks for the wall at the Lake

Shrine. It was then that I first heard from Br. Adolf about Leo, about his search, and how he and his friends planned to go to India. At that time I have just started on Master's path, and everything and everybody was of the greatest interest for me.

I must say that not much has changed in this regard — I still enjoy knowing that others, too, are following in Master's footsteps, each in his own way, loyally and faithfully.

Leo's reminiscences about Master were delightful and enjoyable as ever; sometimes it seems strange that one hears such stories again and again, and still enjoys them like the first time. But, after all, I have listened to Beethoven's Ninth Symphony many, many times, and I still enjoy it with the same intensity. (Although, many years ago when I was still a youngster, and listened to it, conducted by the famous conductor Lovro Matachich, it was just too much and I fainted. I still vividly remember the overwhelming feeling of beauty, before I had passed out!)

We are looking forward to your next visit and, in the meantime, all my good wishes!

In His Love,

Premamoy

Yogananda's protection was never far away from Leo. During their travels, Leo and Marcelle became friends with a Korean waitress at a restaurant they frequented. Their new friend Kwi would see them when they visited her city. Not long after his retirement, Leo had a near fatal aneurysm. His medical team later told him that only 10% of those with his condition survive it. Though aware of and grateful for his guru's intercession, Leo had a long recovery time. Marcelle was unable to care for him herself and asked Kwi if she would come and assist her. Kwi agreed and helped nurse him through a complete and full recovery.

Later, it was Marcelle's turn to require assistance as the effects of advanced aging caught up with her. Unable to completely care for her, it was Leo's turn to ask Kwi for assistance. Kwi became a full-time caregiver and helped them both improve the quality of their lives during these challenging circumstances. Marcelle passed away in 2006. Her memorial service was conducted by Leo's friend and SRF Minister Brother Bimalananda. A friend who could not attend sent the following letter that was read at the service.

Dear Leo,

I am writing to complete your request to relate the conversation Marcelle and I had a few years ago while you were visiting.

You hadn't slept much the night before (your first night at my place) and Marcelle and I were both up before you as you caught up on sleep. I don't remember exactly how the conversation started, but Marcelle started to share a bit about your life together. She told me how, many years ago, Brother Anandamoy had told her it can be very difficult for an ex monk to live in the world. He told her that there can be a lot of guilt and suffering for those who had been in the ashram and were now out in the world. As Marcelle told me this, her eyes filled with tears. She told me that she didn't want that to happen to you and was determined to do everything she could to prevent it. As she said this, I felt her tremendous compassion and love for you. It was more than the love of a spouse, it was even more than a motherly love. In it, I felt this amazing example of what a spiritual marriage could be-to see this partner looking out for the highest good of the other.

Now it is time to say goodbye to this sweet soul. I will miss her friendship and affection. It did take me a few years to get in synch with her as she always greeted me with the French custom of kissing both cheeks! I always looked forward to her affectionate greeting and will miss that sweet smile and understanding heart.

But, I know that she is now filled with an overpowering joy. Not only is she free of the body, but is enjoying Master's embrace and a grand reunion with her son. On the evening of the day she passed, I felt her joy in spirit and I have not been able to be sad ever since even though I know we will all miss her.

Godspeed dear friend!

THE MASTER'S PROTECTION THROUGH ANY CHANNEL

Before that year was out, Leo faced another health crisis that fully illustrated Yogananda's protection. In December 2006, Leo was standing with Kwi outside on their driveway. He hadn't been feeling particularly well and had been drinking a lot of fruit juice. One of their neighbors stopped to talk and all of the sudden he turned to Leo and said, "Leo, you don't look good. You need to go the Emergency Room right now!"

Leo said he was "OK," but the neighbor wouldn't drop it. Finally Leo closed his eyes, raised them to the point between the eyebrows, and waited until he felt Master there. He asked his Guru, "Should I go to the Emergency Room?"

He received an immediate "Yes, go ahead and go."

When they arrived at the ER, Leo didn't even know why he was there. A friend in the medical community said that patients can go into a diabetic coma when their blood sugar is over 500. When they checked Leo's it was over 800!

He had a rough time but recovered and stayed in the body over 5 more years.

Just as in other aspects of life, Leo could be a difficult as a patient. But the great master provided a caregiver equal to the task. In Kwi, he provided Leo, with one who could meet his needs. They became closer and eventually married a few years after Marcelle left the body.

In 2011, the headwinds that Leo had been fighting with his health , overwhelmed his body's ability to cope. Decades earlier, while he was with the great master in the body, Yogananda had made a significant promise to him. Yogananda had told him that when the time came for Leo to leave the body, Yogananda who would be there to meet him as he made the transition. Those who knew Leo and his relationship with the great avatar knew that promise was kept.

Caring for Leo was Kwi's full-time job. Though she tried to overcome the loneliness of losing her husband, and the vocation of taking care of him, she never really recovered from the loss. During the Christmas holidays in 2012, Kwi suddenly passed away after a brief illness. Though the circumstances of her meeting and caring for Leo and Marcelle were always a mystery to her, she faithfully carried out her task of being the Master's hands and feet in their care.

Brother Bimalananda and Kwi Cocks at an SRF Convocation

LEO'S LAST HUMAN ANGEL

The following story illustrates the Master's appreciation for Kwi, as expressed through the actions of the first disciple Leo met with his Master all those years ago.

When Kwi was first introduced to this path, Leo took her to see the Mother Center and all the Temples he had served at in Southern California. When they were going to Hollywood, he had called Brother

Bhaktananda and arranged to meet. Brother was very even minded and never got excited about anything. But as they pulled into the Hollywood Temple parking lot and got out of the car, they were surprised to see Brother moving rapidly toward them. Leo naturally thought that Brother was headed toward him to greet him. But Brother passed right by Leo and headed right for Kwi. Taking her hands in both of his, Brother smiled and said, "So, you are Leo's little angel!"

There is no doubt about who it was saying "Thank You" to Kwi for all the years of care she had given to Marcelle and then to Leo. It certainly wasn't easy being there twenty-four hours a day, seven days a week for 365 days a year (for years)! Kwi did all this in attunement with Master's wishes and did it well.

Self-Realization Fellowship

Founded in 1920 by Paramahansa Yogananda

February 14, 2009

Mr. Leo E. Cocks
9745 Coffee Ave.
Las Vegas, NV 89147

Dear Leo,

Thank you for your loving greetings at Christmas, and for the remembrance from you and Kwi. I know you have given out of your heart's devotion to Master. How blessed we are to have been drawn to such a one whose life so purely reflected God's light and love. Hold to the awareness of his presence and know that Master is looking after you now, as he always has. We pass through many experiences over the years, but the one constant reality is God and Guru's changeless love. That is what has always sustained me, and I know that you feel the same way. I pray that you may ever feel Their nearness and watchfulness over your well-being.

May God bless you and Kwi with good health and inner happiness. My divine friendship and blessings ever reach out to you.

God love you,

Daya Mata

Sri Daya Mata

SRI DAYA MATA, PRESIDENT
INTERNATIONAL HEADQUARTERS 3880 San Rafael Avenue Los Angeles, California 90065-3298

LEO'S FINAL WORDS OF ADVICE

About one year before Leo left the body (March 2011) he was asked:

Questioner: It's been a pretty full life, at this point. You had the good karma to be in the company of an Avatar, not just an Avatar but a Premavatar. Is there anything you would like to pass on for those who weren't there with Master in the body? For those who may read these words in the future – one-hundred, two-hundred, or even five-hundred years from now? Is there anything you would want to tell them? What's the key to the path? Is there any advice you would like to pass on to those devotees to come in the future?

Leo: Take it all very seriously and practice the stuff that Master gave. It has all been demonstrated by the Master. It is absolute truth, all of these stories and the things that he has given. But you can't tell when you'll see the results.

Part of my meditations since I was with Master are my reliving those experiences with him. I thank him for this, I thank him for that. I also thank him for his presence when I was a teenager—years later I realized his presence had been with me long before I met him physically. I also thank him for knowing many of his great disciples, especially Saint Lynn. He was the greatest of Master's disciples.

My personal feeling was that Master was the greatest one to come to this earth because he has given more. In his thirty years here in America, Yogananda gave thousands of pages in his writings. In his books and in his talks and lessons, he gave more in one incarnation than any avatar I can think of or that I know about.

It is like I visualize him in this big ocean of cosmic consciousness where the waves come in. Once you get in there, you walk into the water a little bit. Once you get a little deeper into the waves, it is like they start taking over your whole body. He was like that to me, he was a big wave. I got more out of his incarnation than any of the other avatars. I don't think they come any greater than him. If that is the only part of God I realize, it is fine with me.

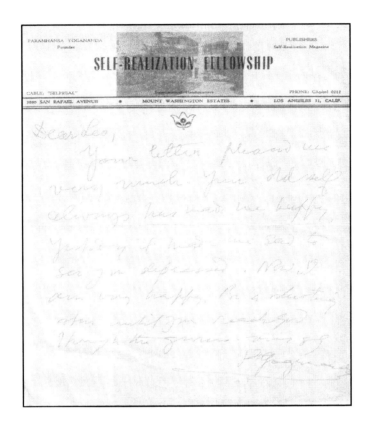

Dear Leo,

Your letter pleased me very much. Your old self has always made me happy. Yesterday it made me sad to see you depressed. Now I am very happy. Be a shooting star until you reach God through the Gurus.

Very sincerely yours,

P. Yogananda

The Master and his notable guests in Encinitas

The boys in the front row (left to right) include:
Bernard, Norman, Leo, Bill, and Steve.

The back row consists of the Uday Shankar family dance troupe
(Ravi Shankar is the young boy on the far right with the garland.) Amelita Galla Curci and
her husband Homer Samuels are pictured left of the Master.

Leo's eyes are closed, as he wishes to stay in tune with his Guru.

Portrait Gallery

These are the people whose names appear in Leo's stories and letters:

Paramahansa Yogananda: Born on January 5, 1893, Yogananda came to the United States in 1920 after years of spiritual study in his native India. He founded Self Realization Fellowship in the USA to spread the spiritual science of Kriya Yoga. His spiritual classic *Autobiography of a Yogi* was published in 1946. Called the Master by his disciples, Yogananda died in Los Angeles on March 7, 1952. Leo joined SRF upon meeting Yogananda in 1948 and was a lifelong member and supporter of SRF. For more information please go to http://yogananda-srf.org.

Sri Daya Mata: The former Faye Wright, Sri Daya Mata entered the SRF ashram in 1931 as a young woman just seventeen years old. She became SRF's third president in 1955. Her life and service have become known as an example of a model spiritual disciple. For more information please go to http://yogananda-srf.org.

Rajarsi Janakananda: Formerly a wealthy businessman named James J. (St.) Lynn, Rajarsi became an exalted disciple of Yogananda. His financial and spiritual support helped put SRF on a firm financial foundation. He advanced quickly in his spiritual life through his ability to listen to Yogananda's spiritual guidance and his own practice of the SRF techniques. Given monastic vows in 1951, he became SRF's second president. For more information please go to http://yogananda-srf.org.

Brother Bimalananda: The former Joe Carbone, Brother Bimalananda was an SRF monk and minister. Brother was a lifelong friend to Leo and presided at the memorial service for Leo's wife Marcelle in 2006.

Brother Premamoy: A senior SRF monk whose life could have been an epic movie. He was a spiritual seeker, a member of European nobility and a resistance fighter in World War II. Brother passed away in 1990 leaving behind a powerful legacy in the many SRF monks he trained during his time as the head of the SRF Postulant Ashram.

Brother Anandamoy: One of the preeminent SRF ministers, Brother and Leo came on the path about the same time in 1948. They had a lasting friendship that reflected their shared love of the great Master. Brother's many talks and videos are available at http://yogananda-srf.org.

Ivan Cocks: Leo's brother Ivan suffered karmic difficulties with mental illness that affected all his family members.

Marcelle Cocks: Leo married Marcelle in 1977 and they were together until her passing in 2006. An SRF member, her quiet spiritual strength was evident to all who knew her.

Dr. and Mrs. Lewis: The Lewis's were two of the earliest disciples of Yogananda in the USA. Their continuing financial support helped Yogananda begin his work in the US and create the Self Realization Fellowship. For more information please go to http://yogananda-srf.org.

Ramakrishna: Vedanta is one of the oldest spiritual philosophies in the world and holds that all religions lead to the same goal. One of the best known Saints that Vedanta produced was Sri Ramakrishna. Leo's family belonged to the Vedanta Society of Northern California.

Mahavatar Babaji: The title means great avatar and Babaji is a supremely advanced master and guru of Lahiri Mahasaya. For more information please go to http://yogananda-srf.org.

Lahiri Mahayasa: This Indian avatar, or embodiment of the divine, was a disciple of Mahavatar Babaji. For more information please go to http://yogananda-srf.org.

Oliver Black: An industrialist from Detroit, Oliver Black met Yogananda and became an advanced householder disciple of SRF.

Known for his joyful spirit, he had a wonderful influence on Leo and his family.

Bernard Cole: During Leo Cocks' ashram years, Bernard was a fellow monk and SRF minister.

Dorothy Taylor: A nun of the Self Realization Fellowship order, Dorothy served as one of Yogananda's secretaries.

Daniel Boone: Leo's friend Daniel Boone was a fellow monk during part of Leo's time with Yogananda in the SRF ashram. Leo considered Daniel a lifelong friend.

Several other SRF monks are identified by name in the photo captions.

CPSIA information can be obtained at www.ICGtesting.com
Printed in the USA
BVOW070036100713

325494BV00003B/248/P